Edexcel GCSE Modular Mathematics

foundation

unit 1

Keith Pledger

Gareth Cole

Peter Jolly

Graham Newman

Joe Petran

www.heinemann.co.uk
✓ Free online support
✓ Useful weblinks
✓ 24 hour online ordering

01865 888058

Heinemann
Inspiring generations

Heinemann is an imprint of Pearson Education Limited,
a company incorporated in England and Wales, having
its registered office at Edinburgh Gate, Harlow, Essex, CM20 2JE.
Registered company number: 872828

Heinneman is a registered trademark of Pearson Education Limited

© Harcourt Education Ltd, 2006

First published 2006

10 09 08
10 9 8 7 6 5 4 3 2 1

British Library Cataloguing in Publication Data is available from the British Library
on request.

ISBN: 978 0 435585 27 3

Copyright notice
All rights reserved. No part of this publication may be reproduced in any form or by any means (including photocopying or storing it in any medium by electronic means and whether or not transiently or incidentally to some other use of this publication) without the written permission of the copyright owner, except in accordance with the provisions of the Copyright, Designs and Patents Act 1988 or under the terms of a licence issued by the Copyright Licensing Agency, Saffron House, 6–10 Kirby Street, London EC1N 8TS. Applications for the copyright owner's written permission should be addressed to the publisher.

Typeset by Tech-Set Ltd, Gateshead, Tyne and Wear
Original illustrations © Harcourt Education Limited, 2006
Cover design by mccdesign
Printed in China (CTPS/01)
Cover photo: Photolibrary.com

Acknowledgements
This high quality material is endorsed by Edexcel and has been through a rigorous quality assurance programme to ensure that it is a suitable companion to the specification for both learners and teachers. This does not mean that its contents will be used verbatim when setting examinations nor is it to be read as being the official specification – a copy of which is available at www.edexcel.org.uk.

The publisher's and authors' thanks are due to Edexcel Limited for permission to reproduce questions from past examination papers. These are marked with an [E]. The answers have been provided by the authors and are not the responsibility of Edexcel Limited.

The authors and publishers would like to thank the following individuals and organisations for permission to reproduce photographs: Getty Images/PhotoDisc pp**1**, **2**, **3**, **7**, **13**, **20**, **27**, **34** bottom, **41**, **45**, **53**, **66**, **71**; Corbis pp**5** top, **6**, **23**, **42**, **43** top, **47**, **50**, **85** top, **85** bottom; Pearson Education Ltd/Debbie Rowe pp**5** bottom, **52**; MorgueFile/Cahilus p**10**; Nature Picture Library/Doug Wechsler p**19**; Empics p**21**; Photos.com pp**24**, **43** bottom, **60**; Pearson Education/Tudor Photograph p**34** top; Pearson Education/Mark Boulton p**38**; iStockPhoto/Ian Francis p**40**; Getty Images/Stone p**65**; Pearson Education Ltd/Jules Selmes p**73**; Pearson Education Ltd/Malcolm Harris p**76**; Digital Vision p**86**

Every effort has been made to contact copyright holders of material reproduced in this book. Any omissions will be rectified in subsequent printings if notice is given to the publishers.

Publishing team
Editorial   Katherine Pate, Jim Newall, James Orr, Evan Curnow, Lindsey Besley,
                  Lyn Imeson, and Elizabeth Bowden
Design   Christopher Howson
Production   Helen McCreath
Picture research Chrissie Martin

Websites
There are links to relevant websites in this book. In order to ensure that the links are up-to-date, that the links work, and that the sites aren't inadvertently linked to sites that could be considered offensive, we have made the links available on the Heinemann website at www.heinemann.co.uk/hotlinks. When you access the site, the express code is **3827P**.

Tel: 01865 888058 www.heinemann.co.uk

Quick reference to chapters

1 Collecting Data — 1

2 Representing and processing data — 13

3 Averages and spread — 27

4 Interpreting data — 40

5 Scatter graphs, correlation and time series — 51

6 Probability — 66

Examination practice paper — 88

Answers — 92

Contents

1 Collecting data

1.1	Introduction	1–2	Types of sample; sources of data	HD1a/2c/5k
1.2	Designing questions	2–4	Writing questions for questionnaires, minimising bias	HD2c/d/e
1.3	Tally charts	4–7	Designing and using data capture sheets	HD3a
1.4	Two-way tables	7–10	Designing and using two-way tables for data capture	HD3c
	Mixed exercise 1	10–11		
	Summary of key points	12		

2 Representing and processing data

2.1	Bar charts and pictograms	13–16	Drawing and interpreting bar charts and pictograms	HD4a/5b
2.2	Pie charts and line graphs	16–19	Drawing and interpreting pie charts and line graphs	HD4a/5b
2.3	Stem and leaf diagrams	20–21	Drawing and interpreting stem and leaf diagrams	HD4a/5b
2.4	Frequency polygons	21–23	Drawing and interpreting frequency polygons	HD4a/5b
	Mixed exercise 2	23–26		
	Summary of key points	26		

3 Averages and spread

3.1	Ungrouped data	27–29	Calculating statistics for small data sets	HD4b/j
3.2	Frequency distributions	29–31	Calculating statistics for discrete frequency distributions	HD4b/g
3.3	Grouped frequency distributions	32–35	Calculating statistics for continuous grouped data	HD4b/g
	Mixed exercise 3	36–39		
	Summary of key points	39		

4 Interpreting data

4.1	Information from tables	40–42	Interpreting databases, tables and mileage charts	HD3b
4.2	Information from graphs and charts	42–45	Interpreting line graphs and bar charts	HD5a/b/c/d

4.3	Comparing data sets	45–47	Comparing distributions using measures of average and spread	HD5a/d
Mixed exercise 4		47–50		
Summary of key points		50		

5 Scatter graphs, correlation and time series

5.1	Scatter graphs and correlation	51–54	Investigating the relationship between two sets of data; correlation and lines of best fit	HD4a/h/5b/c/f
5.2	Time series	54–58	Drawing and interpreting time series	HD4a/5b/j/k
5.3	Retail Price Index	58–61	Interpreting social statistics; calculating prices in line with RPI	HD5k
Mixed exercise 5		61–65		
Summary of key points		65		

6 Probability

6.1	Probability scales	66–69	Representing probabilities on scales labelled in words and numbers; equally likely outcomes	HD4c/5g
6.2	Mutually exclusive outcomes	69–71	Identifying mutually exclusive outcomes; adding simple probabilities	HD4f
6.3	Listing outcomes	71–74	Systematic listing and sample space diagrams	HD4e
6.4	Probability of an event not happening	74–76	P(event does not happen) = 1 − P(event happens)	HD4c
6.5	Estimating likely outcomes	77–78	Predicting results, based on theoretical probability	HD4d/5g
6.6	Estimating probability	78–82	Relative frequency, experimental probability	HD4d/5g
Mixed exercise 6		83–87		
Summary of key points		87		

Examination practice paper
Section A (calculator)   88–89

Section B (non-calculator) 90–91

Answers   92–102

About this book

This book has been carefully matched to the new two-tier modular specification for Edexcel GCSE Maths. It covers everything you need to know to achieve success in Unit 1. The author team is made up of the Chief Examiner, the Chair of Examiners, Principal Examiners and Senior Moderators, all experienced teachers with an excellent understanding of the Edexcel specification.

Key features

Chapters are divided into **sections**. In each section you will find:
- **key points**, highlighted throughout like this

  - You can show continuous data in a **line graph**.

- **examples** that show you how to tackle questions
- an **exercise** to help develop your understanding.

Each chapter ends with a **mixed exercise** and a **summary of key points**. Mixed exercises, which include past exam questions marked with an [E], are designed to test your understanding across the chapter.

Hint boxes are used to make explanations clearer. They may also remind you of previously learned facts or tell you where in the book to find more information.

The mode is the number that occurs most often.

An **examination practice paper** is included to help you prepare for the exam at the end of the unit.

Answers are provided at the back of the book to use as your teacher directs.

Quick reference and detailed Contents pages

Use the thumb spots on the **Quick reference page** to turn to the right chapter quickly.

Use the detailed **Contents** to help you find a section on a particular topic. The summary and reference codes on the right show your teacher the part(s) of the specification covered by each section of the book. (For example, HD3b refers to Handling data, section 3 Collecting data, subsection b.)

Teaching and learning software

References to the *Heinemann* Edexcel GCSE Mathematics **Teaching and learning software** are included for you and your teacher. (The number refers to the relevant chapter from the linear course on which the software is based.)

10 How to collect data

1 Collecting data

1.1 Introduction

- You can collect data:
  - by using a questionnaire
  - by making observations and recording the results
  - by carrying out an experiment
  - from records or a database
  - from the internet.
- Data you collect yourself is called **primary data**. Data that has been collected by other people is called **secondary data**.
- A **census** collects information from every member of a population.
- A **sample** collects information from only part of a population. The larger the sample, the more reliable the results will be.
- When you carry out a survey, select a **random sample** to avoid **bias**.

> 10 How to collect data

> The National Census collects information for every household in the UK. The information is collected every ten years. The next Census will be in 2011.

> In a random sample, every member of the population has an equal chance of being chosen.

Example 1

Brian wants to find out what people think about Heavy Metal music.

He considers asking three different groups of people.

Group A: The people in his class
Group B: The people at a Heavy Metal concert
Group C: The people at a school fete

Which group of people should he ask?

Group C

In group A, Brian would be finding out what people in his own age group think about Heavy Metal music. The people in this group are unlikely to be representative of people in general. In group B the people like Heavy Metal music! They are not representative of people in general.

> There is likely to be a mix of ages and views in this group.

Exercise 1A

For questions 1–4 select the most appropriate group of people to ask: A, B or C.

1. What people think about snooker
    A: The people in a shopping centre
    B: The people in a youth club
    C: Snooker players

2. What people think about Chinese food
    A: People in a Chinese restaurant
    B: People in a supermarket
    C: Men in a football club

3. If people are in favour of the new road
    A: Car drivers using the road
    B: People without a car
    C: People at the local cinema

4. What people think about the cost of dental care
    A: People in a library   B: Dentists   C: Students

5. Hal is doing a survey of the people in his school.
    (a) Who will he choose if he takes a census?
    (b) Write down one advantage of taking a census.
    (c) Write down one disadvantage of taking a census.

6. Here are some sets of data.
    Decide whether each is primary or secondary data.
    (a) Prices of MP3 players in a catalogue
    (b) Ages of people in your family
    (c) Numbers of households with a PC
    (d) Favourite bands of people in your class
    (e) Local people's views on sports facilities
    (f) GCSE results for a school

1.2 Designing questions

> 10 Designing questionnaires and surveys

- In a survey **bias** can result from:
    - leading questions, which invite a particular answer
    - unclear or ambiguous questions
    - people not answering every question.
- When you are writing questions for a **questionnaire**:
    - be clear what you want to find out and what data you need
    - ask short, simple questions
    - provide tick boxes with possible answers
    - avoid questions which are vague, too personal or may influence the answer.

Example 2

Tony conducts a survey into people's TV viewing habits. In his questionnaire he asks the question
'You enjoy watching soap operas, don't you?'
(a) Explain why this is not a good question to ask.
(b) Write three suitable questions which invite people to provide reasonable information about soap operas.

(a) The question is a poor one because it is leading; it invites a person to answer YES.
(b) Three suitable questions might be:
1. Tick the box which shows most accurately the number of hours (t) you spend each week watching soap operas on TV:

   Do not watch □ $0 < t \leq 1$ □ $1 < t \leq 2$ □ $2 < t \leq 3$ □

   $3 < t \leq 4$ □ $4 < t \leq 5$ □   More than 5 □

2. In this list of soap operas, write the numbers 1, 2 and 3 in the boxes to show your 1st, 2nd and 3rd favourite.

   Next Door to You □   For and Against □
   Abdication Road □   Junction Road □
   Riverside □   Other □
   Westsiders □

3. If you have written a 1, 2 or 3 in the box next to 'Other' in question 2, please write the name of this soap opera here:
   Other is _____

Exercise 1B

1 Shani and Erica carry out a survey on the sweets people eat in the office canteen.
Shani writes the question 'Which sweets do you eat?'
Erica says that this question is too vague.
Write down two ways in which the question could be improved.

2 Jack is designing a survey to find out about people who use an internet cafe near his home. One of the things he wants to find out is how far people have travelled to get to the cafe.

(a) Decide which question below is best to ask. Give two reasons for your decision.
   A   How far have you travelled to get here today?
   B   Where do you live?
   C   Do you live far from here?
   D   Please show me on the map where you have travelled from.

Jack decides to do the survey one Friday evening outside the internet cafe.

(b) Give one reason why this could give a biased sample.

3 Petros wants to find out how teenagers communicate with each other.
He designs a questionnaire.
Here are two of his questions.
The questions are **not** suitable.
For each question, write down a reason why.

(a) Do you prefer to communicate with your best friend by mobile or by email?
   Yes ☐   No ☐

(b) How many email addresses do you have?
   1 ☐   2 ☐   3 ☐   4 ☐

4 Daniel is conducting a survey into the amount of money that teenagers spend on magazines.
He uses this question on a questionnaire.

How much money do you spend on magazines?
£1 ☐   £2 ☐   £3 ☐

Write down **two** things that are wrong with this question.

> **Activity – Pastimes**
> - Design a questionnaire to find out about people's pastimes.
> - Test your questions by asking some of your friends.

1.3 Tally charts

> - When you carry out a survey or an experiment you can use a **data capture sheet** to record your results.
> - Data that can be counted is called **discrete data**.
> - Data which is measured is called **continuous data**.
> - A **tally chart** is a way of recording and displaying data.

10 Data collection sheets
12 Discrete and continuous data
12 Frequency tables

Example 3

Hitesh did a survey of the numbers of calls to the emergency services in his town in one month. Here are his results:

3	9	13	2	7	3
5	1	10	16	3	1
6	8	8	10	11	7
4	1	8	4	11	12

Design a data capture sheet on which this data can be collected.
Record the data on the data capture sheet.

The numbers of calls are discrete data. A suitable data capture sheet is a tally chart with numbers of calls in groups of four.

This gives four groups:
1–4
5–8
9–12
13–16

Numbers of calls	Tally	Frequency
1–4	ЖЖ IIII	9
5–8	ЖЖ II	7
9–12	ЖЖ I	6
13–16	II	2

Remember:
Use ЖЖ to represent 5.

Example 4

The weights in grams of 30 humming-birds are:

6.7 4.2 5.8 6.2 7.1 9.2 3.8 6.7 6.1 5.2
6.8 4.4 6.1 6.5 4.3 5.5 6.9 8.0 7.1 6.6
5.4 7.3 7.7 8.8 6.6 6.0 5.5 6.1 9.3 4.2

Design a data capture sheet and use it to record the data above.

A suitable data capture sheet is a tally chart with weights in groups of 10 g.

$3.0 \leqslant w < 4.0$ includes weights of 3.0 g and over, up to but not including 4.0 g.

Weight, w (kg)	Tally	Frequency
$3.0 \leqslant w < 4.0$	I	1
$4.0 \leqslant w < 5.0$	IIII	4
$5.0 \leqslant w < 6.0$	ЖЖ	5
$6.0 \leqslant w < 7.0$	ЖЖ ЖЖ II	12
$7.0 \leqslant w < 8.0$	IIII	4
$8.0 \leqslant w < 9.0$	II	2
$9.0 \leqslant w < 10.0$	II	2

The smallest weight is 3.8 g.
Start the groups at 3.0 g.

The largest weight is 9.3 g.
End the groups at 10.0 g.

Exercise 1C

1 Which of the following are discrete data and which are continuous?
  (a) The time taken to eat breakfast
  (b) The number of songs on a CD
  (c) The number of bees in a beehive
  (d) The weight of an elephant
  (e) The temperature of a cup of tea

2 David sold 24 DVDs on an internet auction site. He recorded the number of bids for each DVD. Here are his results:

9   15   8   7   9   2
10   5   7   12   8   11
13   6   4   3   19   3
6   17   16   7   9   5

Copy and complete the tally chart for this data.

Number of bids	Tally	Frequency
1–5		
6–10		
11–15		
16–20		

3 The heights of 30 trees, in metres, in a park are recorded:

13.1   8.7   6.8   4.3   5.6   18.1   8.3   14.0   10.8   21.7
22.2   6.0   13.6   3.1   11.5   10.8   15.7   3.7   9.4   8.0
6.4   17.0   7.3   12.8   13.5   12.9   10.0   4.2   16.0   11.5

Copy and complete the frequency table below, using intervals of 5 metres.

Height, h (m)	Tally	Frequency
$0 \leq h < 5$		

Make sure your groups don't overlap.

4 30 people used an off-licence one evening. They bought:

Beer   Wine   Spirits   Wine   Sherry   Wine
Sherry   Sherry   Sherry   Beer   Sherry   Beer
Beer   Beer   Spirits   Spirits Beer   Spirits
Beer   Beer   Beer   Sherry   Sherry   Spirits
Beer   Beer   Sherry   Spirits Beer   Sherry

Copy and complete the table to show this information.

Drink	Tally	Frequency
Beer		
Wine		
Spirits		
Sherry		
		Total 30

5 Here are the midday temperatures, in degrees Celsius, for 40 different towns.

18.6 19.3 21.2 17.8 18.3 18.4 22.8 19.6 18.8 17.2
16.3 17.0 21.4 18.0 16.2 19.1 22.2 18.4 17.9 15.4
15.8 22.5 20.8 21.7 18.9 18.5 17.6 18.3 20.1 20.0
17.6 22.0 21.4 19.3 18.0 16.6 20.1 19.2 20.2 18.3

(a) Design a data capture sheet on which these temperatures could be recorded. Use intervals of 1 degree, starting at 15 °C.

(b) Complete your data capture sheet for this data.

6 Billy's home is near a busy main road. He decides to carry out a survey of the different types of car that travel on the main road. Design a suitable data capture sheet for him to use.

7 Alex and June want to collect information on the type of music downloaded by students in their school.
Draw a suitable data collection sheet for this information.

1.4 Two-way tables

- You can use a **two-way table** to record or display data that is grouped in two categories.

Example 5

A travel company offers three types of holiday:
　　Beach　　Cities　　Lakes and mountains
Customers for these holidays are classified by gender as
　　Male or Female
Design a two-way table to collect and record the data about the choice of holiday for people of each gender.

A suitable table is:

	Beach	Cities	Lakes and mountains	Total
Male				
Female				
Total				

Example 6

This incomplete two-way table shows some information about the numbers of shirts sold on a market stall last week.

	Small	Medium	Large	Total
White		50		120
Red	79	35	27	
Blue	40	45		139
Total	135		135	400

Complete the table.
Looking at the first column, for **small** shirts:
The total number of **small** shirts sold was
$$\text{white} + \text{red} + \text{blue} = 135$$
i.e.   white + 79 + 40 = 135
so   white = 135 − 40 − 79
           white = 16

Then looking across the first row, for **white** shirts:
    small + medium + large = 120
i.e.   16 + 50 + large = 120
so   large = 120 − 50 − 16
                large = 54

Then looking across the second row, for **red** shirts:
    small + medium + large = total
i.e.   79 + 35 + 27 = total
so   total = 141

Then looking down the second column, for **medium** shirts:
    total = white + red + blue
    total = 50 + 35 + 45
    total = 130

Then looking down the third column, for **large** shirts:
    white + red + blue = total
       54 + 27 + blue = 135
              blue = 135 − 54 − 27
              blue = 54

You can check that the fourth column of **totals** add to give 400.
   120 + 141 + 139 = **400** so the values are correct.

The final table is:

	Small	Medium	Large	Total
White	**16**	50	**54**	120
Red	79	35	27	**141**
Blue	40	45	54	139
Total	135	**130**	135	400

Exercise 1D

1 The two-way table gives some information about the lunch arrangements of 85 students.

	School lunch	Packed lunch	Other	Total
Female	21		13	47
Male		5		
Total	40			85

Copy and complete the two-way table. [E]

2 Mary is conducting a survey into the ways students usually travel to school.
She has identified the four methods of travel as:
   Walk   Cycle   Car   Bus

She has also classified the students as:
   KS3   KS4   Sixth form

Design a two-way table Mary could use to collect and record data.

3 Bob asked 100 adults which type of music they enjoyed the most. They could choose Jazz, Rock, Classical or Folk music.

The two-way table shows some information about their answers.

	Jazz	Rock	Classical	Folk	Total
Men	12		19	4	52
Women		23			
Total	21			11	100

Copy and complete the two-way table.

4 A reporter recorded the gender and age of the 35 people at a meeting of the European Parliament in Strasbourg.

Here are her results:

Male 33	Female 24	Female 58	Male 29
Male 48	Male 45	Female 57	Male 44
Male 46	Female 40	Female 49	Male 52
Female 33	Female 37	Female 52	Male 42
Male 54	Male 48	Male 56	Male 52
Male 49	Male 59	Male 56	Female 37
Male 34	Male 49	Male 39	Male 48
Male 49	Male 55	Female 32	Female 29
Male 37	Female 32	Male 50	

The European Parliament have monthly sessions in Strasbourg.

Record the data on a copy of the data capture sheet below.

Age (years)	Male	Female	Total
21–30			
31–40	|		
41–50			
51–60			
Total			35

Hint: Use tallies. This represents one male who is between 31 and 40 years old.

Mixed exercise 1

1 Gary is looking at the mileage of some second-hand cars. No car has completed more than 100 000 miles or less than 10 000 miles.

(a) Design a suitable data capture sheet for the data. Give reasons for your design.

In Gary's first sample of 40 cars, the mileages are:

12 850	23 402	16 011	76 852	57 113
45 206	93 444	15 347	25 143	17 642
56 442	33 449	18 730	42 665	85 472
22 225	43 571	88 432	19 002	52 000
17 036	83 202	66 661	57 349	14 027
95 671	75 420	34 006	23 975	62 510
44 921	48 632	34 285	37 848	26 936
44 502	11 032	63 021	51 128	24 137

(b) Record these values on your data capture sheet.

Mixed exercise 11

2 The maximum and minimum temperatures in degrees Celsius, were recorded one day for 15 different holiday resorts. The results are given in the table below.

Max.	37.1	42.0	16.2	24.1	22.1	17.4	26.7	27.3	29.0	27.4	22.4	18.6	31.7	30.0	33.5
Min.	26.8	27.2	12.1	26.2	14.2	12.3	22.0	19.8	22.1	19.3	13.8	10.5	23.7	22.0	24.7

(a) Design a data capture sheet for these temperatures. Give reasons for your design.

(b) Complete your data capture sheet for these temperatures.

3 Sumreen is doing a survey into how much time students in a school spend each week playing computer games. She is particularly interested to see whether there is any difference between the times for boys and for girls. Design, giving your reasons, a suitable data capture sheet she could use for her survey.

4 A student wanted to find out how many pizzas adults ate. He used this question on a questionnaire.

'How many pizzas have you eaten?'

☐   ☐
A few   A lot

(a) Write down **two** things that are wrong with this question.

He gave his questionnaire to 10 of his teachers.

(b) Give **two** reasons why this is not a good way to find out how many pizzas adults ate. [E]

5 80 students each study one of three languages.

The two-way table shows some information about these students.

	French	German	Spanish	Total
Female				
Male		17		
Total	31	28		80

39 of the 80 students are female.
15 of the 39 female students study French.
Copy and complete the two-way table. [E]

Summary of key points

1. You can collect data:
   - by using a questionnaire
   - by making observations and recording the results
   - by carrying out an experiment
   - from records or a database
   - from the internet.

2. Data you collect yourself is called **primary data**. Data that has been collected by other people is called **secondary data**.

3. A **census** collects information from every member of a population.

4. A **sample** collects information from only part of a population. The larger the sample, the more reliable the results will be.

5. When you carry out a survey, select a **random sample** to avoid **bias**.

6. In a survey **bias** can result from:
   - leading questions, which invite a particular answer
   - unclear or ambiguous questions
   - people not answering every question.

7. When you are writing questions for a **questionnaire**:
   - be clear what you want to find out and what data you need
   - ask short, simple questions
   - provide tick boxes with possible answers
   - avoid questions which are vague, too personal or may influence the answer.

8. When you carry out a survey or an experiment you can use a **data capture sheet** to record your results.

9. Data that can be counted is called **discrete data**.

10. Date which is measured is called **continuous data**.

11. A **tally chart** is a way of recording and displaying data.

12. You can use a **two-way table** to record or display data that is grouped in two categories.

2 Representing and processing data

2.1 Bar charts and pictograms

- You can show discrete data, or data in words, in a **bar chart**. Remember to leave gaps between the bars.

> Examples of data in words are 'red', 'small', 'blond'.

Example 1

Joanne surveys 30 swimmers in her swimming club. She records the colour of each person's swim suit.

Blue	Red	Red	Green	Black	Red	Yellow	Blue
Red	Pink	Red	Red	Blue	Black	White	Red
Yellow	Green	Red	White	Red	Blue	Yellow	White
Red	Blue	Green	Yellow	White	Red		

(a) Complete this tally chart for these results.

Colour	Tally	Frequency
Blue		
Red		
Green		
Black		
Yellow		
Pink		
White		

(b) Draw a bar chart to show this information.

(c) Which is the most common swimsuit colour for the swimming club?

(a)

Colour	Tally	Frequency
Blue	|||||	5
Red	||||| |||||		11
Green	|||	3
Black	||	2
Yellow	||||	4
Pink			1
White	||||	4

> A table that shows the number of times each data value occurs is called a **frequency distribution**.

Chapter 2 Representing and processing data

(b)

[Bar chart: Frequency vs Colour. Blue: 5, Red: 11, Green: 3, Black: 2, Yellow: 4, Pink: 1, White: 4]

> A diagram that shows the number of times each data value occurs is called a **frequency diagram**.

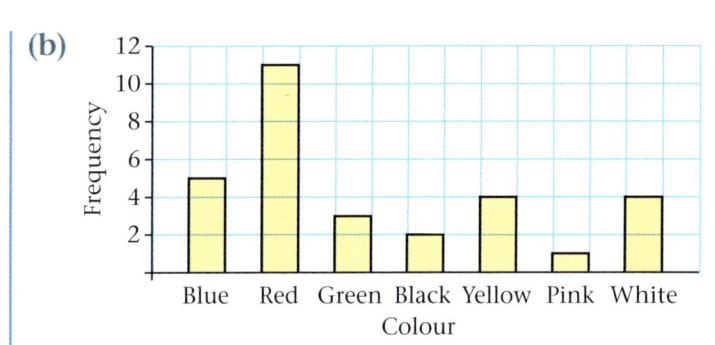

(c) The most common swimsuit colour is the one with the greatest frequency, so it is red.

> Red has the tallest bar in the bar chart and the highest frequency in the tally chart.

Example 2

The bar chart shows some information about the number of megapixels each of four cameras use.

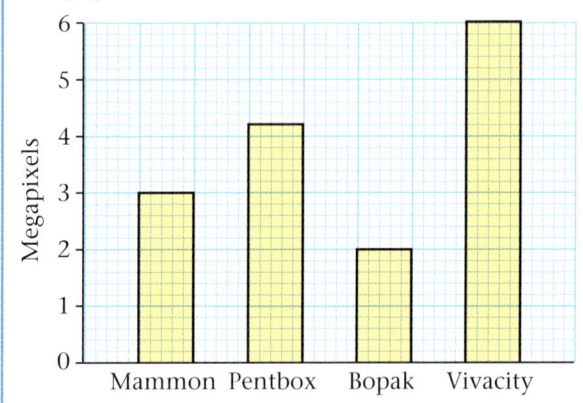

[Bar chart: Megapixels vs camera. Mammon: 3, Pentbox: 4.2, Bopak: 2, Vivacity: 6]

(a) Which camera uses the largest number of megapixels?
(b) Work out the difference in the number of megapixels used between the Mammon and the Pentbox cameras.
(c) An Optickler camera uses 4.8 megapixels. Show this on the bar chart.

(a) Vivacity
(b) $4.2 - 3 = 1.2$ megapixels
(c)

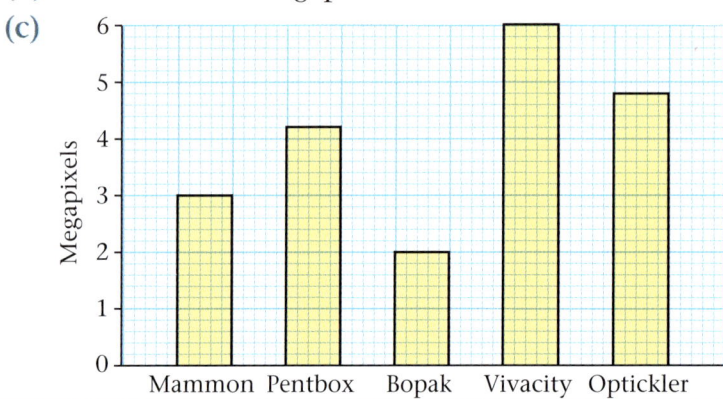

[Bar chart: Megapixels vs camera. Mammon: 3, Pentbox: 4.2, Bopak: 2, Vivacity: 6, Optickler: 4.8]

2.1 Bar charts and pictograms

A pictogram uses symbols or pictures to represent a quantity. It needs a **key** to show what one symbol represents.

Example 3

This pictogram shows the numbers of drivers caught by a speed camera in Askhorne last week.

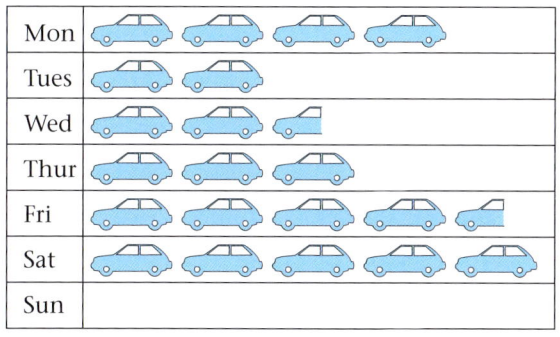

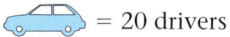

Mon	🚗 🚗 🚗 🚗
Tues	🚗 🚗
Wed	🚗 🚗 🚗½
Thur	🚗 🚗 🚗
Fri	🚗 🚗 🚗 🚗 🚗½
Sat	🚗 🚗 🚗 🚗 🚗 🚗
Sun	

🚗 = 20 drivers

(a) Write down the number of drivers caught by this speed camera
 (i) last Monday (ii) last Wednesday (iii) last Friday.

Last Sunday 30 drivers were caught speeding.
(b) Draw symbols to show this.

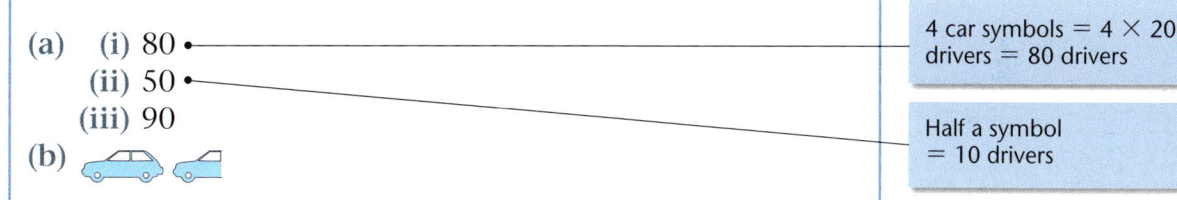

(a) (i) 80 — 4 car symbols = 4 × 20 drivers = 80 drivers
 (ii) 50 — Half a symbol = 10 drivers
 (iii) 90
(b) 🚗 🚗½

Exercise 2A

1 Forty people were asked the make of car they drive.
 Their answers were:

Ford	Skoda	Ford	Vauxhall	Jaguar	BMW	Vauxhall	Ford
BMW	Rover	Vauxhall	Ford	Rover	Fiat	Ford	Fiat
Rover	Ford	Ford	Vauxhall	Ford	Jaguar	Vauxhall	Ford
Ford	Vauxhall	Rover	Ford	BMW	Fiat	Honda	Honda
Rover	Ford	Ford	Honda	Ford	Jaguar	Ford	Ford

 (a) Draw and complete a tally chart for this information.
 (b) Draw a bar chart for this information.
 (c) For these 40 people, which is the most popular make of car?

2 The pictogram shows the number of swimmers who used the swimming pool on four days last week.

Sun	🏊 🏊 🏊
Mon	🏊 🏊 🏊 🏊
Tues	🏊 🏊
Wed	

🏊 = 10 swimmers

(a) How many swimmers used the swimming pool last Sunday?
(b) How many swimmers used the pool last Monday?
(c) On Wednesday 35 swimmers used the swimming pool. Draw symbols to show this.

3 The bar chart shows some information about the numbers of prescriptions a doctor gave in four days.

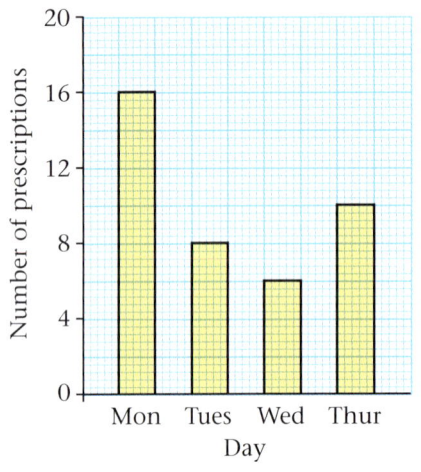

(a) On which day did the doctor give the smallest number of prescriptions?
(b) How many more prescriptions did the doctor give on Monday than on Thursday?

On Friday the doctor gave 14 prescriptions.
(c) Copy and complete the bar chart.
(d) Work out the total number of prescriptions the doctor gave in the week.

2.2 Pie charts and line graphs

- A **pie chart** shows how something is shared or divided.
- The angles at the centre of a pie chart add up to 360°.

20 Drawing pie charts
20 Interpreting pie charts

2.2 Pie charts and line graphs

Example 4

The table shows the amount of oil used per day by five countries.

Country	Barrels of oil per day (millions)
United States	20
China	6
Japan	5
Russia	3
UK	2
Total	36

Draw a pie chart to show this information.

On the pie chart, the angle for the United States will be:

$$\frac{20}{36} \times 360 = 200°$$

Total number of barrels = 36
The US share is $\frac{20}{36}$
There are 360° in the whole pie chart.

The other angles are:

China: $\frac{6}{36} \times 360 = 60°$

Japan: $\frac{5}{36} \times 360 = 50°$

Russia: $\frac{3}{36} \times 360 = 30°$

UK: $\frac{20}{36} \times 360 = 20°$

So the pie chart is:

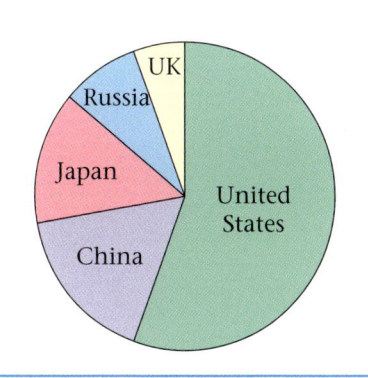

Example 5

The pie chart shows the proportions of people with blood groups A, O, B and AB. The data is for 500 people living in Weymouth.

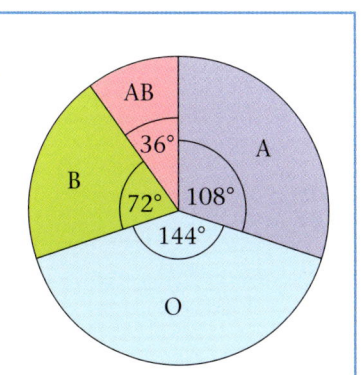

(a) Which blood group is most common?
(b) How many people were in each blood group?

AB 36°, A 108°, B 72°, O 144°

(a) O is the most common blood group.
(b) The pie chart represents 500 people.
The angle for blood group O is 144°.
So the number of people with blood group O is
$\frac{144}{360} \times 500 = 200$ people

For the other blood groups:
Blood group A: $\frac{108}{360} \times 500 = 150$ people
Blood group AB: $\frac{36}{360} \times 500 = 50$ people
Blood group B: $\frac{72}{360} \times 500 = 100$ people

Check:
200 + 150 + 50 + 100 = 500 which is the correct total.

- You can show continuous data in a **line graph**.

A line graph that illustrates data collected at timed intervals (hourly, daily, weekly, etc.) is called a **time series**. There is more about time series graphs in Chapter 5.

Example 6

The table shows a baby's weight in kg over 6 weeks. Draw a line graph to show this information.

Week	1	2	3	4	5	6
Weight (kg)	2.4	2.2	2.4	2.7	2.9	3.2

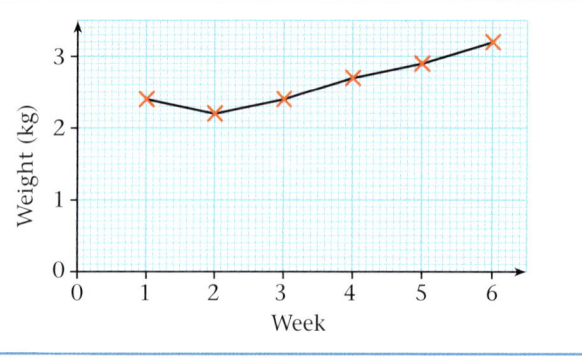

Exercise 2B

1 Harry collected data on the food some people bought in the restaurant today. Here are his results:

Food	Frequency
Pizza	5
Chicken tikka	12
Fish and chips	10
Baked potato	3

(a) Draw a bar chart to show this information.
(b) Show the information on a pie chart.

Use squared paper.

2. Sixty people used a sports centre one evening.
   They each took part in only one of the following activities:

   Aerobics   Badminton   Football   Squash   Tennis

   The pie chart shows information about their activities.
   (a) Which of the activities was most popular?
   (b) How many of the 60 people took part in aerobics?
   (c) What fraction of the 60 people took part in football?

3. The table gives some information about which supermarket 90 people shopped in.

Supermarket	Frequency	Angle
Whiteways	36	
Baldy	18	
Miniver's		
Fine Fare		
Total	90	

   (a) Use the information in the table to copy and complete the pie chart.
   (b) Use the information in the pie chart to copy and complete the table.
   (c) Which of these four supermarkets is
       (i) most popular   (ii) least popular?

4. Draw a pie chart for the car data in Exercise 2A question **1**.

5. The table shows the depth of water in a pond over an eight-week period.
   Copy the axes and draw a line graph to show this information.

Week	1	2	3	4	5	6	7	8
Depth (cm)	24	21	29	23	17	26	30	25

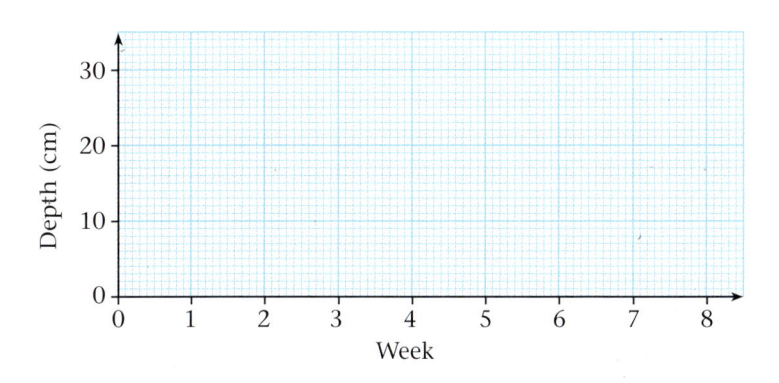

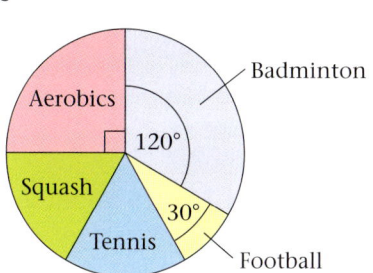

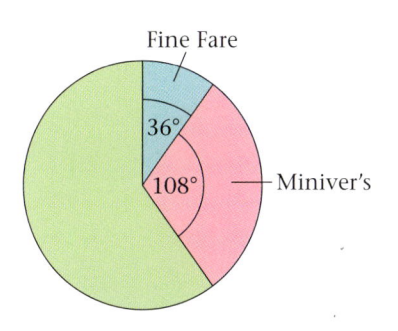

   There are over 5000 known species of frog worldwide.

2.3 Stem and leaf diagrams

> 20 Drawing stem and leaf diagrams

- A **stem and leaf diagram** shows the shape of a distribution and keeps all the data values. It needs a **key** to show how the stem and leaf combine.

Example 7

The 30 students in Set 2 take a Science test marked out of 50. Their marks are given below.

32	41	17	24	43	36	47	12	26	32
45	16	9	22	35	27	28	20	37	34
19	7	18	26	33	29	48	37	25	23

Using the tens as the stem, represent this information as a stem and leaf diagram.

```
0 | 7 9
1 | 2 6 7 8 9
2 | 0 2 3 4 5 6 6 7 8 9
3 | 2 2 3 4 5 6 7 7
4 | 1 3 5 7 8
```

Key: 4 | 1 means 41

The stems are 0, 10, 20, 30 and 40.

Remember to give a key.

Exercise 2C

1 Here are Shinai's ten-pin bowling scores:

43	32	64	85	71	38	57	52	63	51
91	77	62	72	55	54	62	67	80	49
51	63	70	63	44	48	64	57	62	72
54	57	42	55	61	90	66	61	50	69

Represent this information as a stem and leaf diagram.

2 Carly did a survey into the ages of people using a library one day. Here are her results.

27	25	17	32	8	36	57	49	82	61
64	70	19	12	44	38	29	20	16	22
46	51	54	73	34	38	61	48	46	49
52	56	29	26	31	64	54	59	50	33
41	32	27	46	52	6	15	46	42	38
48	53	52	45	39	33	42	40	61	56

(a) Draw stem and leaf diagram to show these ages.

(b) Carly says 'There were more library users in their 60s than any other age group.' Is she correct?

3 The heights in cm of 30 athletes are recorded below:

170 167 172 185 159 176 186 179 168 201
164 191 182 183 169 177 173 186 183 192
149 181 171 169 173 184 188 173 179 168

Draw a stem and leaf diagram to show this data.

2.4 Frequency polygons

- You can show grouped continuous data in a **histogram**. A histogram has no gaps between the bars.
- A **frequency polygon** shows the general pattern of data in a histogram.

Example 8

The table shows the weekly rainfall, in millimetres, for one year.

Rainfall per week, r (mm)	Frequency
$0 \leq r < 5$	8
$5 \leq r < 10$	6
$10 \leq r < 15$	17
$15 \leq r < 20$	10
$20 \leq r < 25$	7
$25 \leq r < 30$	4

Draw a frequency polygon for this frequency distribution.

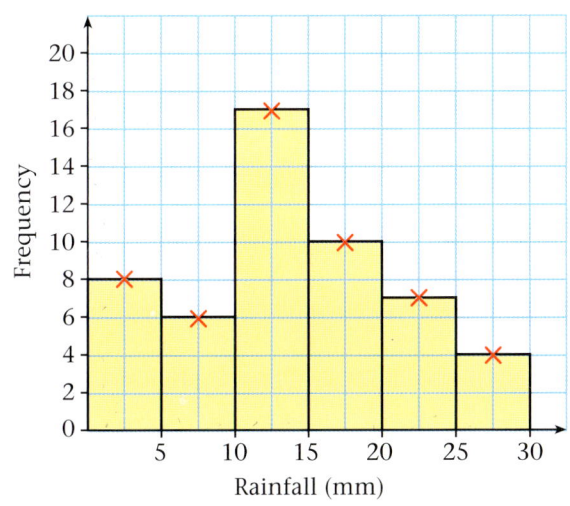

1. Draw the histogram.
2. Mark the mid-points of the bars.

Chapter 2 Representing and processing data

3. Join the mid-points of the bars.

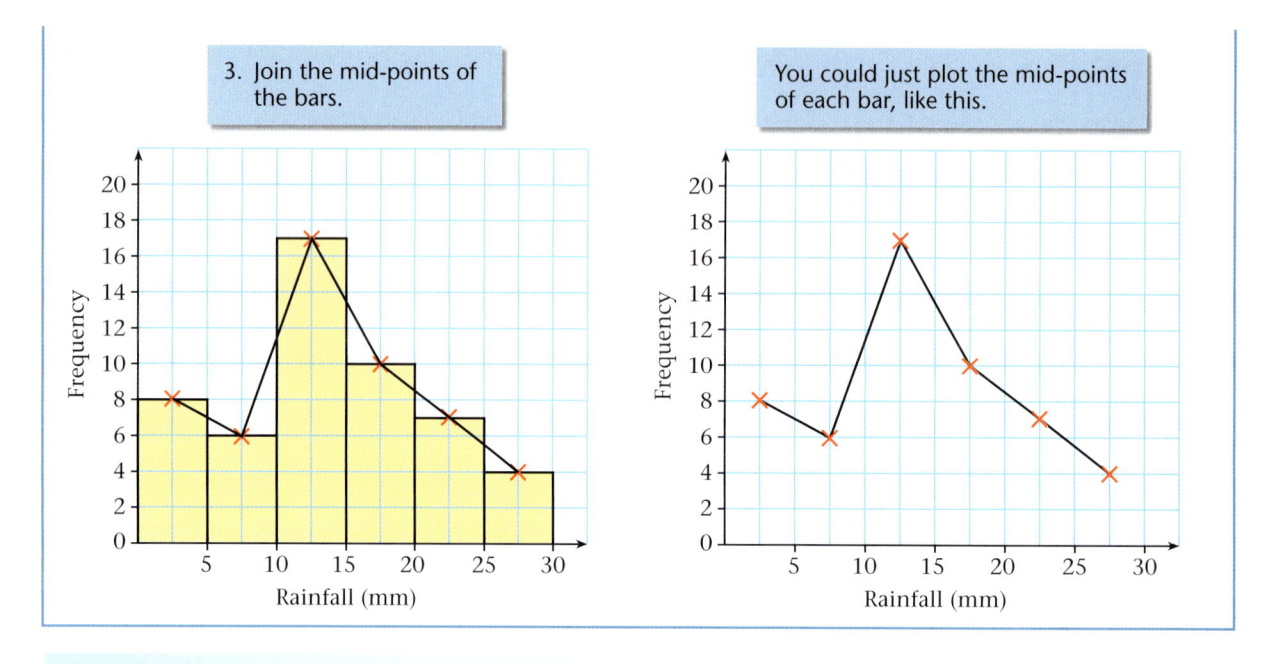

You could just plot the mid-points of each bar, like this.

Exercise 2D

1. The police recorded the speeds of 100 vehicles on a dual carriageway. The results are shown in the table below.

Speed, s (mph)	Frequency
$20 < s \leq 30$	8
$30 < s \leq 40$	12
$40 < s \leq 50$	19
$50 < s \leq 60$	22
$60 < s \leq 70$	30
$70 < s \leq 80$	6
$80 < s \leq 90$	3

Represent this information as a frequency polygon.

2. The table shows the times, in minutes, for some people to complete a puzzle.

Time, t (minutes)	Frequency
$20 < t \leq 30$	8
$30 < t \leq 40$	12
$40 < t \leq 50$	16
$50 < t \leq 60$	14
$60 < t \leq 70$	10

Draw a frequency polygon to show this information.

3 The sizes of fish in a lake are recorded. The distribution of lengths of the fish is given in the table below.

Length, l (mm)	Frequency
$0 < l \leqslant 100$	2
$100 < l \leqslant 200$	8
$200 < l \leqslant 300$	15
$300 < l \leqslant 400$	10
$400 < l \leqslant 500$	5

Show this information as a frequency polygon.

Activity – Investigating height
- (Go to www.heinemann.co.uk/hotlinks, insert the express code 3827P and click on this activity.)
- Use the Mayfield database to select at random the heights of 50 students from Key Stage 4 (KS4).
- Record the data in a frequency table using the class intervals $1.3 \leqslant h < 1.4$, $1.4 \leqslant h < 1.5$, etc.
- Draw a frequency polygon for this information.
- Comment on the shape of your frequency polygon.

Mixed exercise 2

1 Forty people are asked their favourite type of music. Their answers are:

Pop   Classical   Jazz   Rock   Pop   Jazz
Pop   Rock   Pop   Pop   Jazz   Rock
Rock   Pop   Pop   Rock   Jazz   Pop
Pop   Rock   Rock   Classical   Pop   Pop
Jazz   Jazz   Rock   Pop   Rock   Pop
Pop   Classical   Pop   Rock   Rock   Pop
Pop   Pop   Jazz   Rock

(a) Copy and complete the tally chart and frequency table.

Type of music	Tally	Frequency

(b) Draw a bar chart to show this information.
(c) Draw a pie chart for this information.

2 The pictogram shows the number of diamond rings sold by a shop in January, February and March.

January	⊕ ⊕ ⊕
February	⊕ ⟓
March	⊕ ⊕
April	
May	

Key ⊕ represents 4 diamond rings.

(a) Write down the number of diamond rings sold in January.
(b) Work out how many **more** diamond rings were sold in March than in February.

20 diamond rings were sold in April.
14 diamond rings were sold in May.

(c) Copy the pictogram. Use this information to complete it.

3 200 people were asked when and where they took their summer holiday: in the UK, Europe or elsewhere.
The incomplete table shows some of their responses.

	UK	Europe	Elsewhere	Total
July		20	8	40
August	36		16	
September		32		60
Total	56	100		

France is currently the world's most popular foreign holiday destination.

(a) Copy and complete the table.
(b) Draw a pie chart to represent the total numbers of people holidaying in each of the three months.
(c) Draw a second pie chart to represent the total numbers of people holidaying in the UK, Europe or elsewhere.

4 The table gives the share price of a company on the first ten days in one month.

Day	1	2	3	4	5	6	7	8	9	10
Share price (pence)	23	23	26	22	28	32	29	30	26	32

Copy and complete the line graph to show this information.

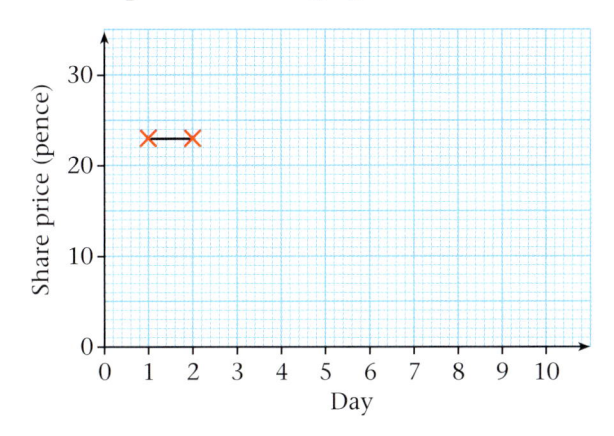

5 The monthly average midday temperatures are recorded in the table below.

Month	Temperature (°C)
October	−5
November	−17
December	−22
January	−24
February	−19
March	−11
April	−1
May	9

Represent this information as a line graph.

6 The pie chart provides some information about the colours of 120 cars in a car park.
Copy the frequency table.
Use the information from the pie chart to complete it.

Colour	Frequency

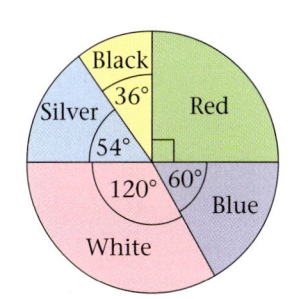

7 The table shows information about the heights of Christmas trees in a garden centre.

Height, h (cm)	Frequency
$50 < h \leq 90$	7
$90 < h \leq 130$	15
$130 < h \leq 170$	12
$170 < h \leq 210$	5
$210 < h \leq 250$	3

Represent this information as a frequency polygon.

8 There are 27 boxes in a warehouse. The frequency polygon for their weights is shown opposite.

Represent this information as a frequency table.

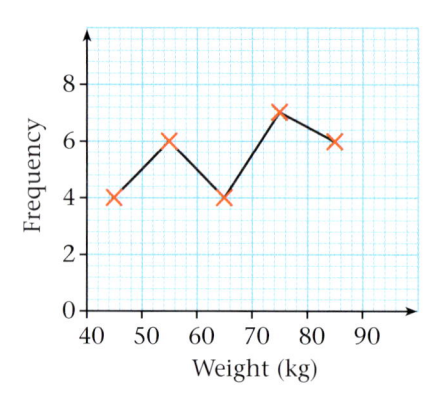

9 The costs per night, in £, for a double room in 24 hotels are:

110 118 125 110 134 132 169 125
127 141 110 111 120 149   99 159
120 125 127 180 163 170 109 115

Represent this information as a stem and leaf diagram.

Summary of key points

1 You can show discrete data, or data in words, in a **bar chart**. Remember to leave gaps between the bars.

2 A **pictogram** uses symbols or pictures to represent a quantity. It needs a **key** to show what one symbol represents.

3 A **pie chart** shows how something is shared or divided.

4 The angles at the centre of a pie chart add up to 360°.

5 A **stem and leaf diagram** shows the shape of a distribution and keeps all the data values. It needs a **key** to show how the stem and leaf combine.

6 You can show grouped continuous data in a **histogram**. A histogram has no gaps between the bars.

7 A **frequency polygon** shows the general pattern of data in a histogram.

3 Averages and spread

3.1 Ungrouped data

- The **mode** of a set of data is the value which occurs most often.
- The **median** is the middle value when the data is arranged in order of size.
- The **mean** of a set of data is the sum of the values divided by the number of values:

  $$\text{mean} = \frac{\text{sum of values}}{\text{number of values}}$$

- The **range** of a set of data is the difference between the highest value and the lowest value:
  range = highest value − lowest value
- The **modal class** is the group which has the highest frequency.

> 20 Introducing the median
> 20 Calculating the median

Example 1

Here are the numbers of nuclear reactors in each of ten non-European countries:

  2 14 53 2 16 104 2 3 2 1

(a) Find the mode.
(b) Find the median.
(c) Work out the mean.
(d) Work out the range.

(a) The mode is 2.

(b) Putting the numbers in order of size gives
  1 2 2 2 2 3 14 16 53 104
There are two middle values, 2 and 3,
so the median is $\frac{2+3}{2} = \frac{5}{2} = 2.5$ nuclear reactors.

The mode is the number that occurs most often.

The median is the mean of the two middle values.

(c) Mean $= \dfrac{2 + 14 + 53 + 2 + 16 + 104 + 2 + 3 + 2 + 1}{10}$
  $= \dfrac{199}{10} = 19.9$ nuclear reactors

(d) Range = highest value − lowest value
  = 104 − 1 = 103

Chapter 3 Averages and spread

Example 2

The stem and leaf diagram shows the number of complaints received by a television broadcasting company for each of 20 programmes.

```
0 | 2, 4, 5, 6, 8
1 | 0, 2, 2, 3, 5, 7, 7, 9
2 | 1, 1, 8, 8, 8, 8
3 | 0
```

Key: 3|0 means 30 complaints

11th value (points to the 7 in row 1)
10th value (points to the 5 in row 1)

(a) Find the mode.
(b) Find the median.
(c) Work out the range.

(a) The mode is 28.
(b) The median is the $\frac{20 + 1}{2}$ = 10.5th value = 16
(c) The range is 30 − 2 = 28

The average of the 10th and 11th values is
$\frac{15 + 17}{2} = 16$

Example 3

The frequency diagram shows the distribution of ages for the population of Madwell village.
Write down the modal class for these ages.

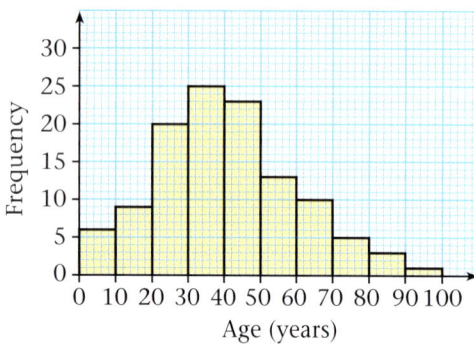

The modal class is the age group 30 to 40.

Exercise 3A

1 Here are the numbers of nuclear reactors in each of nineteen European countries:

   27 13   5 11   9   1   6 30   1   1
    2   4 19 59   4   6   6   7   1

   (a) Find the mode.
   (b) Find the median.
   (c) Work out the mean.
   (d) Work out the range.

2 Last term Jenny did 14 homeworks in History.
Her marks were

$8\frac{1}{2}$ 7 6 8 4 5 5 9 8 8 4 $8\frac{1}{2}$ $7\frac{1}{2}$ $5\frac{1}{2}$

(a) Find the mode of these marks.
(b) Find the median of these marks.
(c) Work out the mean mark.
(d) Work out the range of these marks.

3 Here are the times, in minutes, of 10 films:

162 174 155 132 201 188 175 168 146 187

(a) Find the median time.
(b) Work out the range of the times.
(c) Work out the mean time.

4 The stem and leaf diagram shows the number of tree rings in each of 25 tree stumps.

```
2 | 5 5 5 5 6 8 9 9
3 | 0 0 2 2 6 7 7 8
4 | 3 3 5 7 7 8 8        Key: 5|1 means 51 tree rings
5 | 1 3
```

Find
(a) the mode
(b) the median
(c) the range.

5 Use the 'mean' function on your calculator to work out the mean of the numbers

3 7 8 5 9 10 7 8 6 2

Check your results without using a calculator.

The key may be labelled $\overline{X}$ or $\overline{x}$

6 The grouped frequency diagram shows the distribution of the weights of a group of people.
Write down the modal class interval.

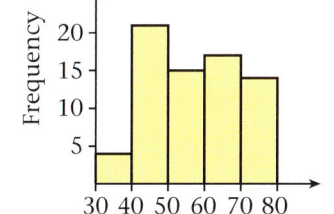

3.2 Frequency distributions

- When n values are written in ascending order:
  the median is the $\frac{n+1}{2}$th value.
- For a frequency distribution: mean $= \frac{\Sigma fx}{\Sigma f}$

Example 4

In a survey, Helen recorded the number of yogurts her friend ate on one particular weekend.
The results are shown in the table.

Number of yogurts, x	Frequency, f
0	4
1	11
2	6
3	4
Total	25

Work out
(a) the mode
(b) the median
(c) the mean
(d) the range.

(a) The mode is the value which occurs most often. In a frequency table this is the item of data with the highest frequency.
For this data the highest frequency is 11, for 1 yogurt.
The mode is 1 yogurt.

(b) The 25 data values in the table are written in ascending order. So the median value is
the $\frac{n+1}{2}$th = $\frac{25+1}{2}$ = 13th value.
The 13th person in the table ate 1 yogurt.
The median is 1 yogurt.

Number of yogurts, x	Frequency, f	Frequency × number of yogurts, f × x
0	4	0
1	11	11
2	6	12
3	4	12
Totals	$\Sigma f = 25$	$\Sigma fx = 35$

Mean = $\frac{\Sigma fx}{\Sigma x}$

= $\frac{35}{25}$ = 1.4 yogurts

(d) Range = 3 − 0
= 3 yogurts

Number of yogurts, x	Frequency, f
0	4
1	11

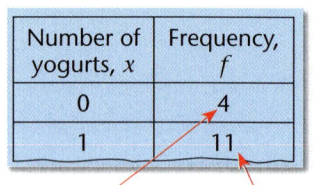

1st–4th people ate 0 yogurts
5th–15th ate 1 yogurt

Σ means 'the sum of'.
Σf = the sum of all the f values.
f × x is written fx.

Exercise 3B

1 The table shows the number of goals scored by Halifax Wanderers in 20 matches.

Work out
(a) the mode
(b) the median
(c) the mean.

Copy the table and add an $f \times x$ column.

Number of goals, x	Frequency, f
0	5
1	6
2	7
3	1
4	1
Total	20

2 The table shows the number of days lost through illness in April for 47 employees in a company.

Days	0	1	2	3	4
Frequency	27	9	6	3	2

Work out
(a) the range
(b) the mean.

3 In a survey, Ross asks some people about the number of brothers and sisters that they each have. The table shows his results.

Brothers and sisters	0	1	2	3	4	5
Frequency	11	20	13	3	2	1

Work out
(a) the mode
(b) the mean.

4 The table shows information about the number of people living in each of 100 houses.

Number of people, x	Frequency, f
1	5
2	13
3	20
4	25
5	19
6	11
7	7
Total	100

Work out
(a) the mode
(b) the mean
(c) the range.

3.3 Grouped frequency distributions

- For grouped data:
  - you can state the class interval that contains the median
  - the class interval with the highest frequency is called the **modal class**
  - you can calculate an estimate of the mean using the middle value of each class interval.

Example 5

The table provides information about the amount of rain that fell during the 52 weeks of one year.

Amount of rain, r (mm)	Number of weeks
$0 \leq r < 5$	8
$5 \leq r < 10$	6
$10 \leq r < 15$	17
$15 \leq r < 20$	10
$20 \leq r < 25$	7
$25 \leq r < 30$	4

Work out an estimate for the mean amount of rain that fell per week.

Add columns for the middle values (x) of the intervals and $f \times x$.

Rainfall	Middle value of interval (x)	Frequency (number of weeks, f)	$f \times x$
0 to <5	2.5	8	$8 \times 2.5 = 20$
5 to <10	7.5	6	$6 \times 7.5 = 45$
10 to <15	12.5	17	$17 \times 12.5 = 212.5$
15 to <20	17.5	10	$10 \times 17.5 = 175$
20 to <25	22.5	7	$7 \times 22.5 = 157.5$
25 to <30	27.5	4	$4 \times 27.5 = 110$
		$\Sigma f = 52$	$\Sigma fx = 720$

Mean $= \dfrac{\Sigma fx}{\Sigma f}$

$= \dfrac{720}{52} = 13.846$

The mean amount of rain per week is 13.85 mm (to 2 d.p.).

From the table, the maximum amount of rain is 30 mm and the minimum is 0 mm. So, as a rough guess, the mean is likely to be about halfway between 0 and 30, which is 15 mm.

Example 6

The frequency distribution shows the ages of 49 members of an aerobics class.

Age, a (years)	Frequency
$10 < a \leq 20$	4
$20 < a \leq 30$	18
$30 < a \leq 40$	10
$40 < a \leq 50$	14
$50 < a \leq 60$	3

(a) Write down the modal class interval for the ages.

(b) Work out which class interval contains the median age.

(c) Work out an estimate for the mean of the ages.

(d) Work out the maximum possible range for the ages.

(a) The modal class is $20 < a \leq 30$ years.

This is the group with the highest frequency.

(b) The data in the table is in order. There are 49 people altogether.

The median value is the $\frac{n+1}{2}$th = $\frac{49+1}{2}$ = 25th value.

The interval $30 < a \leq 40$ contains the 25th value.

(c)

Age, a	Middle value of interval (x)	Frequency (f)	f × x
$10 < a \leq 20$	15	4	60
$20 < a \leq 30$	25	18	450
$30 < a \leq 40$	35	10	350
$40 < a \leq 50$	45	14	630
$50 < a \leq 60$	55	3	165
		$\sum f = 49$	$\sum fx = 1655$

Mean = $\frac{\sum fx}{\sum f}$

= $\frac{1655}{49}$ = 33.8 years correct to one decimal place.

(d) The lowest possible age is 10 years. The highest possible age is 60 years.
So the maximum possible range is 60 − 10 = 50 years.

Exercise 3C

1. The frequency table gives information about the number of text messages that Gina received each day in a month.

Number of text messages	Frequency
0 to 2	8
3 to 5	13
6 to 8	6
9 to 11	3
12 to 14	1

165 million text messages in the UK were sent on Jan 1st 2006.

(a) Write down the modal class interval.

(b) Work out the class interval which contains the median.

(c) Calculate an estimate for the mean number of text messages per day.

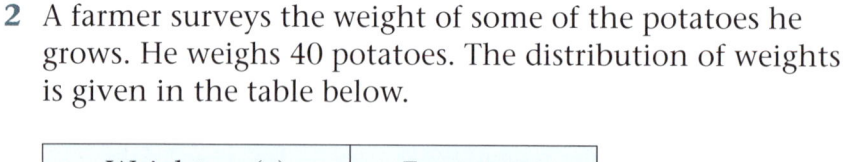

2. A farmer surveys the weight of some of the potatoes he grows. He weighs 40 potatoes. The distribution of weights is given in the table below.

Weight, w (g)	Frequency
$0 < w \leqslant 100$	2
$100 < w \leqslant 200$	16
$200 < w \leqslant 300$	10
$300 < w \leqslant 400$	9
$400 < w \leqslant 500$	3

(a) Work out an estimate for the mean weight of the potatoes.

(b) Write down the class interval which contains the median weight.

(c) Write down the modal class interval.

(d) Write down the maximum possible range for the weight of the potatoes.

3 A survey is conducted on the speeds of 80 vehicles on a main road at lunchtime. The results of the survey are:

Speed (s) in mph	Frequency
$0 < s \leqslant 10$	1
$10 < s \leqslant 20$	2
$20 < s \leqslant 30$	10
$30 < s \leqslant 40$	30
$40 < s \leqslant 50$	32
$50 < s \leqslant 60$	3
$60 < s \leqslant 70$	2

(a) Work out an estimate for the mean speed of these vehicles.

(b) Write down the modal class interval for the speed.

(c) Write down the class interval which contains the median.

The speed limit on the road is 45 mph.

(d) Estimate how many of the vehicles in the survey were exceeding the speed limit. Give your reasons.

Activity – Estimating the mean (an investigation)

Here are the times, in seconds for each of 50 people to complete a number puzzle:

80	65	57	30	61	91	67	61	86	51
38	44	81	40	63	45	86	33	67	88
65	81	94	41	55	94	52	53	75	58
86	57	35	65	64	31	53	97	61	85
47	85	49	56	46	93	60	68	47	68

1 Draw a grouped frequency table for this data. Use class intervals $30 \leqslant x < 40$, $40 \leqslant x < 50$, etc.

2 Use your grouped frequency table to calculate an estimate for the mean time to complete the number puzzle.

3 Repeat **1** and **2** using class intervals $30 \leqslant x < 45$, $45 \leqslant x < 60$, etc.

4 Repeat **1** and **2** using other equal, smaller class intervals, e.g. $30 \leqslant x < 40$, $40 \leqslant x < 50$, etc.

5 Calculate the actual mean of the times.

6 Comment on your findings.

Mixed exercise 3

1. Here are the number of cases of malaria that Dr Chang saw each month, for a year.

    11   20   14   19   10   7   11   17   12   16   9   15

    (a) Work out the median.

    (b) Work out the range.

2. The stem and leaf diagram shows information about the areas of 32 photographs.

    ```
    0 | 8 8 9
    1 | 1 1 3 4 4 8 9
    2 | 0 3 5 5 7 8 8 9
    3 | 2 2 3 3 5 6 8 8
    4 | 1 1 3 3 5 8           Key: 4|1 represents 41 cm²
    ```

    (a) Write down the number of photographs that have an area of 38 cm².

    (b) Work out the median. [E]

3. Amanda collected 20 leaves and wrote down their lengths, in cm.

    Here are her results.

    5   6   5   2   4   5   8   7   5   4
    7   6   4   3   5   7   6   4   8   5

    (a) Copy and complete the frequency table to show Amanda's results.

Length in cm	Tally	Frequency
2		
3		
4		
5		
6		
7		
8		

    (b) Write down the modal length.

    (c) Work out the range. [E]

4 The midday temperatures, in °C, in 25 holiday resorts are shown below:

24 23 19 28 20 31 38 32 27 29 18 26 27
23 30 26 29 33 28 26 26 28 21 20 25

(a) Copy and complete the table for these temperatures.

Temperature, T (°C)	Tally	Frequency
$15 \leq T < 20$		
$20 \leq T < 25$		
$25 \leq T < 30$		
$30 \leq T < 35$		
$35 \leq T < 40$		

(b) Find the median temperature.
(c) Find the modal class interval.
(d) Work out the mean of the temperatures.

5 The mean of five numbers is 8.
Four of the numbers are 7, 9, 10, 3.
(a) Work out the fifth number.
(b) Find the median of the five numbers.

6 Rosie had 10 boxes of drawing pins.
She counted the number of drawings pins in each box.
The table gives information about her results.

Number of drawing pins	Frequency
29	2
30	5
31	2
32	1

(a) Write down the modal number of drawing pins in a box.
(b) Work out the range of the number of drawing pins in a box.
(c) Work out the mean number of drawing pins in a box.   [E]

7 The speeds, in mph, of 30 motorbikes on a motorway are:

44 42 60 55 81 72 75 48 56 68
59 75 72 69 80 50 52 66 71 68
73 56 62 58 63 60 64 37 88 73

(a) Work out the mean speed of these motorbikes.
(b) Find the median speed.

(c) Work out the range of the speeds.
(d) Copy and complete the frequency table.

Speed (s) in mph	Tally	Frequency
$30 \leqslant s < 40$		
$40 \leqslant s < 50$		
$50 \leqslant s < 60$		
$60 \leqslant s < 70$		
$70 \leqslant s < 80$		
$80 \leqslant s < 90$		

(e) Write down the modal class interval for the speed.

8 There are 15 children in a choir.
Ten of the children are girls and five of the children are boys.
The mean age of the girls is 9.2 years.
The mean age of the boys is 7.4 years.
Work out the overall mean age of the 15 children.

9 The distribution of the ages, in years, of 60 women diagnosed with breast cancer is represented by the frequency diagram.
(a) In which class interval does the median age lie?
(b) Write down the modal class interval.

10 The number of people attending a Duke of Edinburgh's scheme was recorded over 28 weeks.
The highest number attending was 18 and the range was 8.
The group leader worked out that the mean number of people attending was 8.7.
Explain why the group leader's calculation for the mean number must be incorrect.

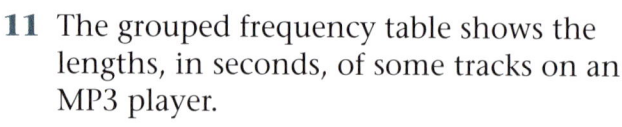

11 The grouped frequency table shows the lengths, in seconds, of some tracks on an MP3 player.
Samir works out an estimate for the mean time of the tracks.
He works out the answer to be 2840 seconds.
Without working out an estimate for the mean, explain why Samir's answer must be incorrect.

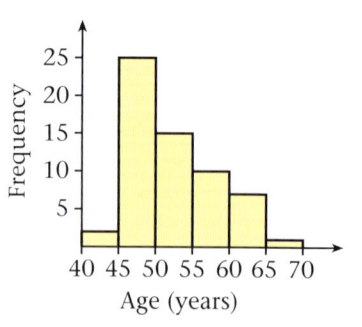

Time, t (seconds)	Frequency
$0 < t \leqslant 100$	4
$100 < t \leqslant 200$	16
$200 < t \leqslant 300$	25
$300 < t \leqslant 400$	14
$400 < t \leqslant 500$	1

12 Bill recorded the times, in minutes, taken to complete his last 40 homeworks.

The table shows information about the times.

Time, t (min)	Frequency	
$20 \leq t < 25$	8	
$25 \leq t < 30$	3	
$30 \leq t < 35$	7	
$35 \leq t < 40$	7	
$40 \leq t < 45$	15	

(a) Find the class interval in which the median lies.

(b) Calculate an estimate of the mean time it took Bill to complete each homework. [E]

Summary of key points

1 The **mode** of a set of data is the value which occurs most often.

2 The **median** is the middle value when the data is arranged in order of size.

3 The **mean** of a set of data is the sum of the values divided by the number of values:

$$\text{mean} = \frac{\text{sum of values}}{\text{number of values}}$$

4 The **range** of a set of data is the difference between the highest value and the lowest value:

range = highest value − lowest value

5 The **modal class** is the group which has the highest frequency.

6 When n data values are written in ascending order the median is the $\frac{n+1}{2}$th value.

7 For a frequency distribution the mean = $\frac{\Sigma fx}{\Sigma f}$

8 For grouped data:
- you can state the class interval that contains the median
- the class interval with the highest frequency is called the **modal class**
- you can calculate an estimate of the mean using the middle value of each class interval.

You do not know the individual data values. So you can only calculate an **estimate** for the mean.

4 Interpreting data

4.1 Information from tables

- A **database** is an organised collection of information. It can be stored on paper or on a computer.

Example 1

Here is an extract from a computer database.

Country	Capital city	Highest mountain	Height (m)	Longest river	Length (km)	Currency
France	Paris	Mont Blanc	4807	Loire	1006	Euro
Germany	Berlin	Zugspitze	2963	Rhine	1320	Euro
Italy	Rome	Mont Blanc	4807	Po	652	Euro
Spain	Madrid	Pico del Teide	3478	Ebro	925	Euro
Sweden	Stockholm	Kebnekaise	2111	Klara-Göta	720	Krona
UK	London	Ben Nevis	1343	Severn	354	Pound

Use the database to answer the following questions.
(a) What is the capital city of Spain?
(b) Which countries do not have the euro?
(c) Which country has the longest river?
(d) Which countries have a mountain over 4000 m high? Comment on your answer.

(a) Madrid
(b) Sweden and the UK
(c) Germany
(d) France and Italy. It is the same mountain (Mont Blanc is on the border).

To answer questions like these using a computer database, you can use the program search tools.

Example 2

Here is a mileage chart.
Use the mileage chart to work out the distance between Cardiff and Salisbury.

```
Bristol
44    Cardiff
120   153   London
73    107   56    Oxford
52    98    85    70    Salisbury
```

Follow the arrows from Cardiff and Salisbury to find where they meet.
The distance between Cardiff and Salisbury is 98 miles.

Activity – Country facts database

Copy the database from Example 1 into a spreadsheet.
Find information about other countries to add to your database.

Remember: When you collect data from the internet make sure the data comes from a reliable source and that the data is accurate – check against other sources.

Exercise 4A

1 The table below is an extract from a travel company's advertisement for summer holidays.

Place	Month	Duration	Method of travel	Cost
Austria	August	14 days	Coach	£365
Majorca	August	7 days	Fly	£399
Tenerife	July	14 days	Fly	£650
Costa Brava	June	7 days	Coach	£199
Paris	June	3 days	Rail	£159
Barcelona	July	3 days	Fly	£269
Sorrento	July	14 days	Fly	£599
Minorca	June	14 days	Fly	£450
Capri	August	7 days	Fly	£859
Edinburgh	July	4 days	Rail	£249

When it was built in 1889 the Eiffel Tower was the tallest structure in the world at 300 m high.

(a) Write down the cost of a 14-day holiday to Sorrento in July.
(b) Peter can afford to spend a maximum of £300 on his holiday.
Write down the names of all the places from the above list he can afford to visit.
(c) Which two places could you go to by coach?
(d) Amy must take her holiday in August. She can only take a maximum of seven days and can afford no more than £500. Which is the only place she can visit?

2 The table shows the marks that six students received in some recent tests.

	English	Science	Mathematics
Gary	52	61	48
Fiona	73	34	69
Asif	55	73	67
Sumreen	57	68	83
Jane	81	66	72
Philip	56	39	47

(a) Who has the highest mark in Mathematics?

(b) Who has the lowest mark in Science?

The pass mark in English was 56.

(c) Who *did not* pass English?

3 Here is a mileage chart.

The distances on the chart are all in miles.

Athens				
1199	Baghdad			
693	796	Cairo		
3110	1960	2736	Delhi	
5310	4259	5048	2344	Hong Kong

(a) Work out the distance
   (i) between Athens and Delhi
   (ii) between Hong Kong and Baghdad.

(b) Which two cities are the closest together?

(c) Which two cities are the furthest apart?

(d) Simon travels from Athens to Cairo, then from Cairo to Delhi, and then from Delhi to Athens. How far does he travel in total?

4.2 Information from graphs and charts

- **Line graphs** can be used to show **continuous data**.

Example 3

Tony's pulse rate was taken every 6 hours over 3 days.
The graph shows his pulse rate in beats per minute.

(a) Write down
   (i) Tony's lowest pulse rate during these three days
   (ii) when the pulse rate was recorded.

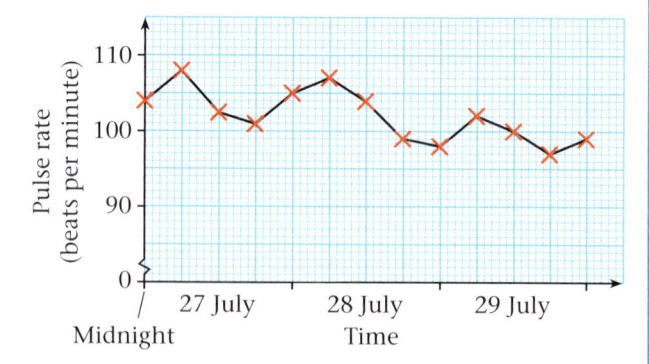

(b) Work out the difference between his highest and lowest pulse rates on 27th July.

(a) (i) The lowest pulse rate was 97 beats per minute.
    (ii) It was recorded at 6 pm on 29th July.

(b) On 27th July the highest and lowest recorded pulse rates were 108 and 101 beats per minute. The difference between these values is
    $108 - 101 = 7$ beats per minute

- You can compare sets of data represented in line graphs or bar charts.

4.2 Information from graphs and charts   43

Example 4

The line graphs show the average midday temperatures in England and Gibraltar for April to October.
Write three comments about these graphs.

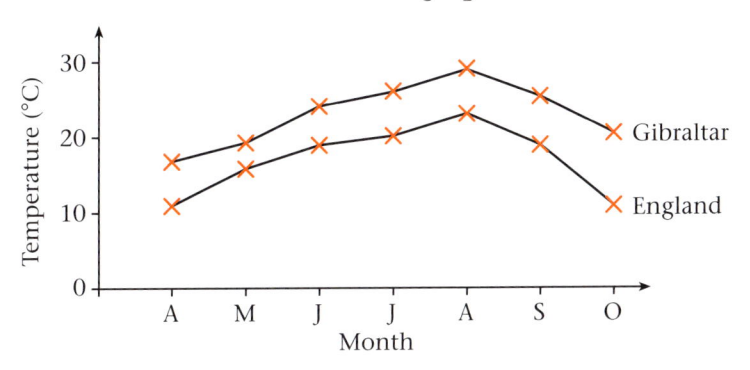

The Rock is Gibraltar's most famous feature. It is 426 metres high.

(i) The temperature in Gibraltar is consistently higher than the temperature in England.
(ii) The month when the temperature difference between Gibraltar and England is at its lowest is May.
(iii) The month when the temperature difference between Gibraltar and England is at its greatest is October.

Example 5

The diagram shows the maximum and minimum depths of a river over seven months.

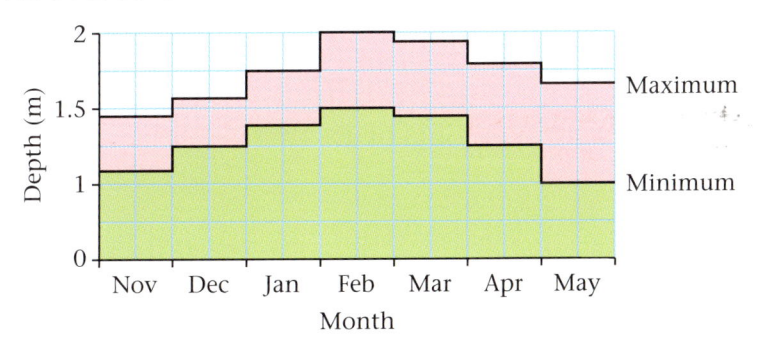

(a) During which month was the river's depth greatest?
(b) During which month was the difference between the maximum and minimum depths of the river the greatest?

(a) The greatest depth, of 2 metres, was in February.
(b) The greatest difference between the maximum and minimum depths of the river was in May.

Look for the tallest bar.

Look for the biggest difference between the two coloured sections.

Exercise 4B

1. The graphs below show information about the value of two cars over an eight-year period.
   The engine sizes of the cars are 2000 cc and 1200 cc.

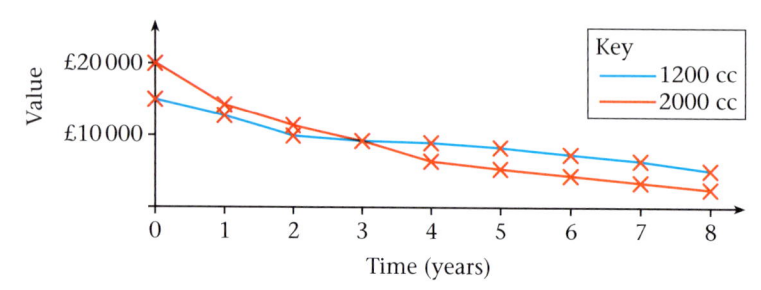

   Key
   — 1200 cc
   — 2000 cc

   Write three comments about the relative prices of these two cars over the eight-year period.

2. The graphs below show information about the variation in average house prices in regions **A** and **B** over a ten-year period.

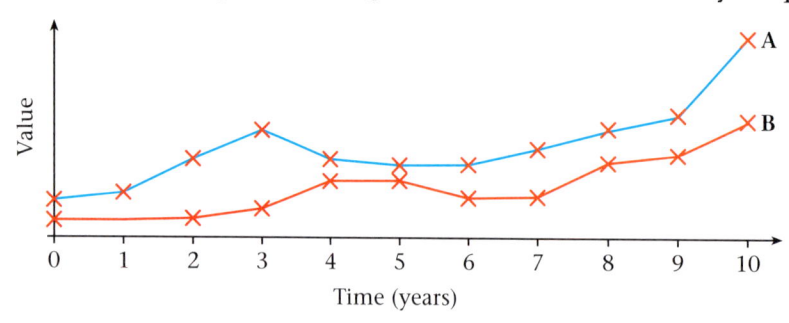

   Comment as fully as possible on the information shown in the graphs.

3. Here is a bar chart showing the number of hours of TV that Helen and Robin watched last week.

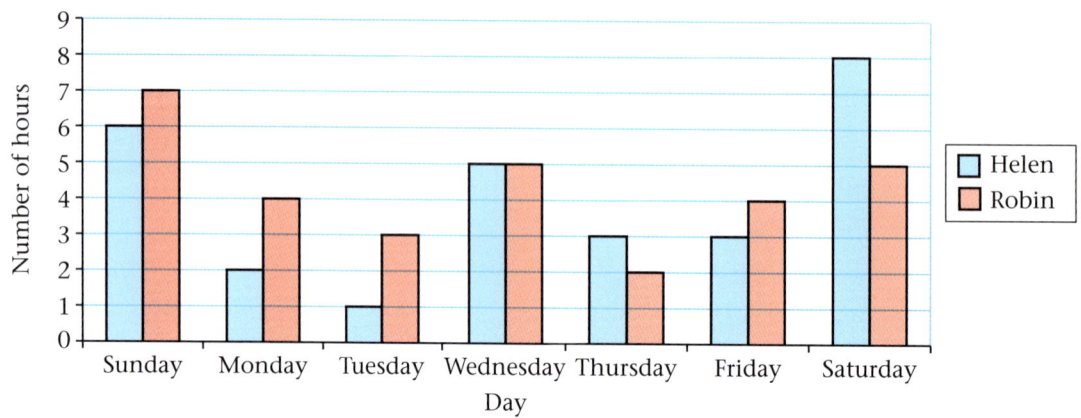

   (a) Write down the number of hours of TV that Helen watched on Monday.

(b) On which day did Helen and Robin watch the same number of hours of TV?
(c) (i) Work out the total number of hours of TV that Robin watched on Friday and Saturday.
(ii) Who watched the greater number of hours of TV on Friday and Saturday?
Show your working. [E]

4 The bar charts show the temperatures in London and Barcelona during the summer months.

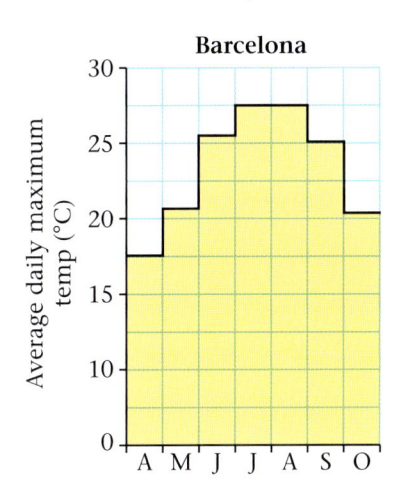

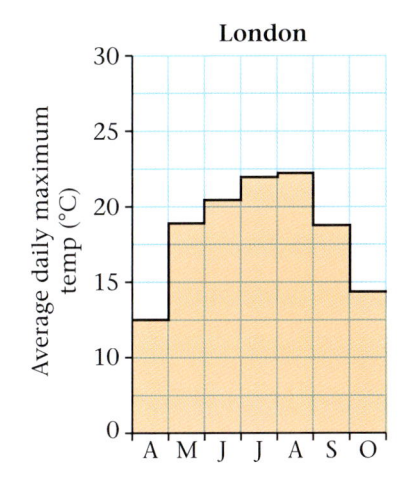

Las Ramblas in Barcelona is one of the most famous streets in the world.

(a) During which month is the temperature at its highest in London?
(b) Work out the difference between temperatures in London and Barcelona during May.
(c) Write a comment comparing the temperatures in Barcelona and London.

4.3 Comparing data sets

- You need a measure of average *and* a measure of spread to compare two sets of data.

The mean, mode and median are measures of average.

The range is a measure of spread.

Example 6

There are 15 girls and 15 boys in class 11T.
They took a spelling test with a maximum mark of 20.

The median mark for the girls was 16, with a range of 4.
The median mark for the boys was 12, with a range of 10.

By comparing the results explain whether the girls or the boys did better in the spelling test.

By just comparing the medians it looks as if the girls, on the whole, did better than the boys.
However, taking the ranges into account and given a maximum mark of 20 it could be possible that several boys scored higher than the maximum mark for the girls.
So the evidence is inconclusive about whether the girls or the boys did better.

Median for girls = 16
Median for boys = 12

Example 7

A group of men and a group of women took their driving theory test.
The average mark for the men was 50.
The average mark for the women was 60.

Explain, using an example if you wish, why it is not possible to say that, in general terms, the women did better in the test than the men.

Only a measure of average is given. To make a full and accurate comparison we need a measure of average and a measure of spread, such as the range.

Without both of these we cannot make a real comparison.

Suppose there were three men and three women.
The marks for the women were 55, 60 and 65.
The marks for the men were 70, 70 and 10.

The mean for the women is then $\dfrac{55 + 60 + 65}{3} = 60$

The mean for the men is then $\dfrac{70 + 70 + 10}{3} = 50$

So the average (mean) for the women is 60, which is greater than the average of 50 for the men.

But it is not possible to say that the women have, in general, done better than the men, because two-thirds of the men scored higher than all the women.

Exercise 4C

1. Mrs Rogers gave her class a mental arithmetic test.
   The median mark for the boys was 7 and the range of the marks for the boys was 4.
   The median mark for the girls was 6 and the range of the marks for the girls was 8.
   Explain whether the boys or the girls did better in this mental arithmetic test.

2 A company researched a new product. It asked a group of girls and a similarly sized group of boys to rate the product. The average rating given by the girls was higher than the average rating given by the boys.
Explain whether or not it is possible to conclude that, in general, the girls rated the product higher than the boys.

3 In a game of golf the person with the lowest score wins.
Nick and Tiger play five games of golf. Here are their scores.

    Nick: 67   74   66   67   66
    Tiger: 64   68   74   67   72

Who is the better player?
Give a reason for your answer.

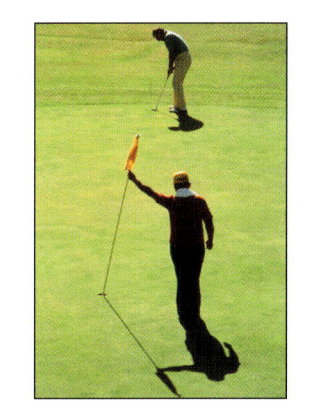

Mixed exercise 4

1 The table shows the distances in kilometres between some cities in the USA.

Boston					
1589	Chicago				
4891	3366	Los Angeles			
2474	2184	4373	Miami		
342	1352	4539	2133	New York	
5067	3493	667	4990	4826	San Francisco

(a) Write down the distance between Los Angeles and New York.

One of the cities in the table is 2184 km from Miami.
(b) Write down the name of this city.
(c) Write down the name of the city which is furthest from San Francisco. [E]

2 The incomplete table and bar chart shows some information about the leisure activities of 100 people.

	Male	Female
Meal out	60	64
Cinema	52	47
Night club		
Spectator sports	31	13

(a) Copy the table. Use the bar chart to complete it.
(b) Copy the bar chart. Use the table to complete it.

3 The mean weekly wage at Spencer and Sons is £210.
The mean weekly wage at Creswell Ltd is £250.
Is it fair to say that the people at Creswell Ltd are better paid than the people at Spencer and Sons? Explain your answer.

4 The graph shows the number of ice creams sold each day during one week.

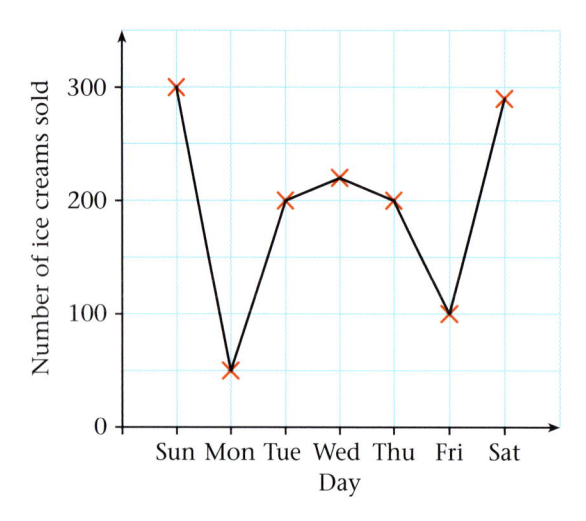

(a) How many more ice creams were sold on Tuesday than on Monday?

(b) Explain what might have happened on Monday. [E]

5 For a project on the prices of used cars, Gary collects information about the prices of two different makes of car. He records the data in two frequency polygons:

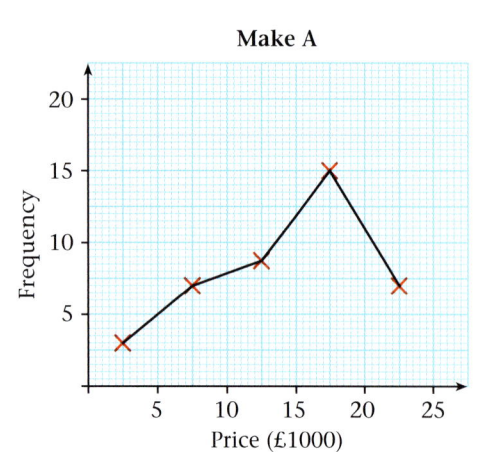

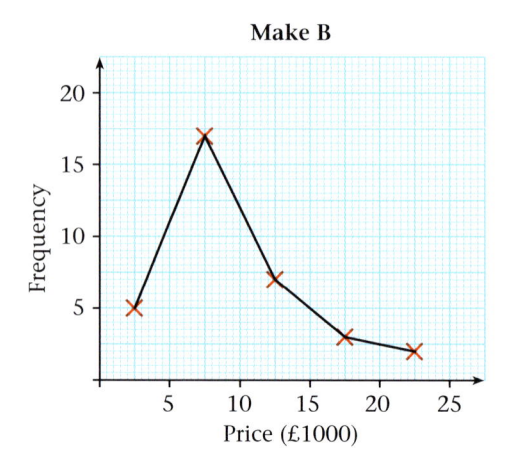

Compare, as fully as possible, the prices of the two makes of car.

6 The table below shows the pass rates (as percentages) for GCSE English in summer 2004 and summer 2005 at High School.

	A*	A	B	C	D	E	F	G	U
2004	3%	12%	21%	24%	18%	17%	3%	2%	0%
2005	2.8%	13.2%	23%	22%	17%	16%	3%	3%	0%

Make three valid comments about these pass rates.

7 Ali and Nick both sell second-hand cars.
Information about the values of the cars they have for sale is shown on the two frequency polygons.

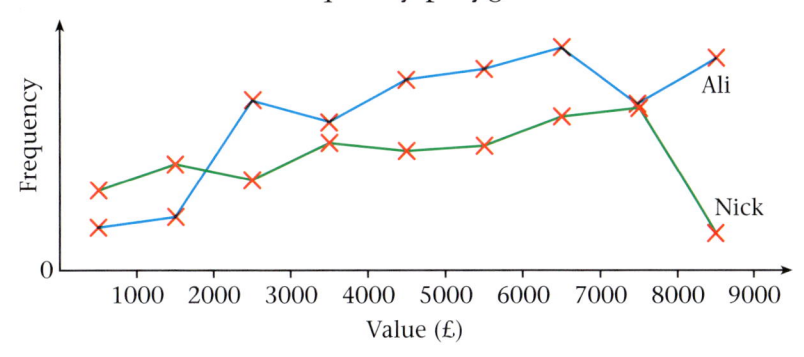

Make three valid comments comparing the values of the cars Ali has for sale with those that Nick has for sale.

8 Dominique asked 72 people at her school their shoe size.
Here are her results.

```
 7  4  5  6  7  4  3  5  5  7  8
 5  3  6  6  6  4  5  4  5  8  9
 5  6  6  5  6  7  6  5  4  4  5
 6  6  6  5  3  9 11  6  7  8  6
 6  8  4  9 10  8  6 10  7  7  7
 4  4 10  9  7  8  6  5  4  3 11
10  9  6  5  6  5
```

(a) Draw a tally chart and frequency table for this data.
(b) Represent the data on a bar chart.
(c) Represent the data on a pie chart.
(d) What is the mode of the shoe sizes?

Dominique's friend did a survey of shoe sizes in another school. She told Dominique that at the other school the mode of the shoe sizes was 7.

(e) Explain whether or not there is sufficient evidence to suggest that the students at the other school have, in general, larger feet than the students at Dominique's school.

9 During the summer of 2002, 32 countries took part in the finals of the football World Cup.
Correct to the nearest million and in millions, the populations of those countries at the time of the World Cup were:

38	10	176	16	1348	4	4	5
13	59	82	4	58	127	49	100
147	5	10	142	22	10	2	45
41	9	10	70	60	287	3	39

(a) Which of these population figures could be described as *exceptional*? Give your reasons.

(b) Explain whether the **mean**, **mode** or **median** would truly reflect the average population of a country taking part in the World Cup finals.

(c) Represent the population figures on a **stem and leaf** diagram.

The first World Cup final took place in 1930. The table below shows the countries that have subsequently won the World Cup, the number of times each country has won it and the population (in millions) of each country.

Country	Number of wins	Population
Brazil	5	176
Italy	4	58
Germany	3	82
Argentina	2	38
Uruguay	2	3
England	1	60
France	1	59

(d) Explain why this data gives the people of Uruguay every right to feel proud of their country's achievement in the World Cup.

Uruguay's independence was recognised in 1828.

Summary of key points

1 A **database** is an organised collection of information. It can be stored on paper or on a computer.

2 **Line graphs** can be used to show continuous data.

3 You can compare sets of data represented in line graphs or bar charts.

4 You need a measure of average *and* a measure of spread to compare two sets of data.

5 Scatter graphs, correlation and time series

5.1 Scatter graphs and correlation

> 24 Plotting scatter diagrams

- A linear relationship between two sets of data is called a **correlation**.

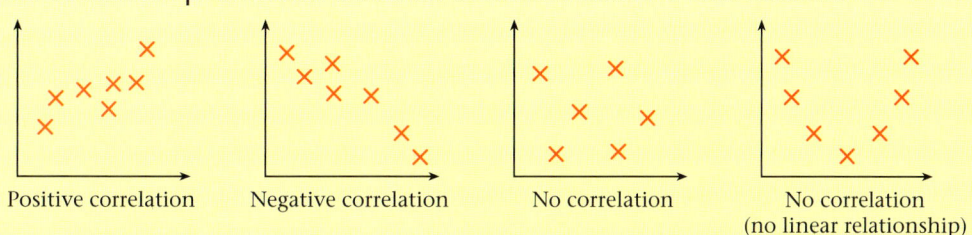

Positive correlation   Negative correlation   No correlation   No correlation (no linear relationship)

- The **line of best fit** is a straight line that passes through or is as close to as many of the plotted points as possible.
- A line of best fit gives a model for how two variables are related. The closer the plotted points are to the line the better the correlation.
- A line of best fit can be used to estimate other data values.

Example 1

The table shows the total hours of sunshine and the total rainfall in mm, in seven towns last summer.

Sunshine (hours)	660	465	550	430	615	400	630
Rainfall (mm)	12	20	16	20	13	28	15

These values are plotted as points on the scatter graph below.

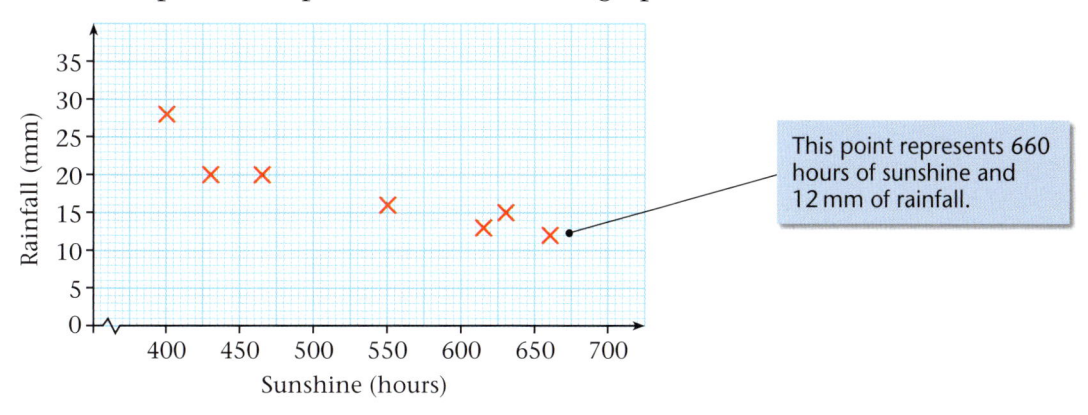

This point represents 660 hours of sunshine and 12 mm of rainfall.

The hours of sunshine and rainfall in three other towns are shown in this table.

Sunshine (hours)	Rainfall (mm)
380	30
525	19
625	35

(a) Plot these extra pairs of values on the scatter graph.
(b) Describe the relationship between the hours of sunshine and the rainfall.
(c) Draw the line of best fit on the scatter graph.
(d) Use your line to find estimates of
   (i) the rainfall in a town with 500 hours of sunshine
   (ii) the number of hours of sunshine in a town that had 15 mm of rainfall.

(a) The complete scatter graph with the three extra points is

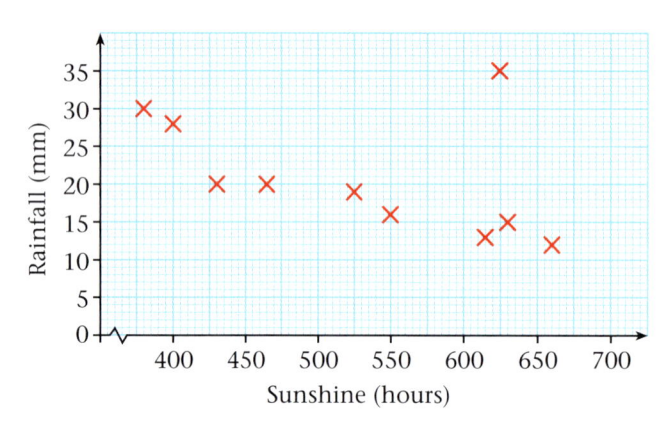

(b) The scatter graph shows that there is negative correlation. As hours of sunshine increase, rainfall decreases.

(c) The line of best fit is as shown.

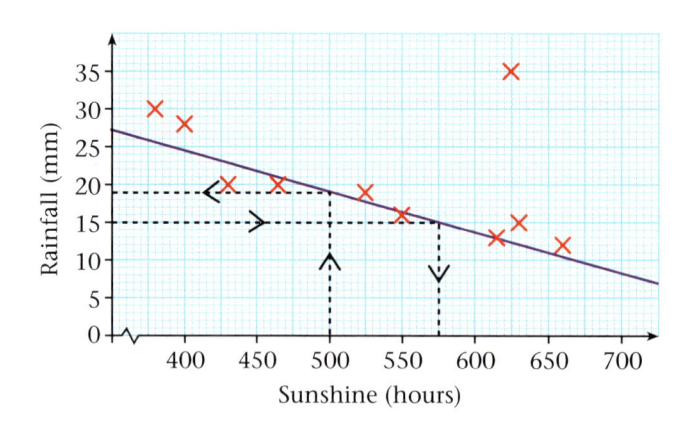

When drawing the line of best fit the point at (625, 35) was ignored. This point is so far from the other data points it is an **exception**. The pattern of weather in this town appears to be different to the other towns. It could perhaps be in a different country.

The points are close to the line of best fit. This shows strong correlation between the amount of sunshine and the amount of rainfall.

(d) The estimates from the line are
   (i) 500 hours gives a rainfall figure of 19 mm
   (ii) 15 mm of rain gives a sunshine figure of 575 hours.

5.1 Scatter graphs and correlations

Exercise 5A

1 Jade sells second-hand cars.
  The table gives the value and mileage of eight cars on his forecourt.

Value (£)	6300	4200	8500	9500	2700	1850	3300	8200
Mileage	24 000	43 000	12 000	6500	94 000	101 000	51 000	14 000

  (a) Plot these values as points on a scatter graph.
  (b) Comment on the correlation between mileage and value.
  (c) Draw a line of best fit on the scatter graph.
  (d) Use your line of best fit to work out an estimate of
      (i) the likely mileage for a car valued at £5000
      (ii) the likely value of a car with a mileage of 72 000.

2 Kieran has conducted a survey examining the heights and weights of some of the people in his rowing club.
  The results for six people are shown in the table below.

Height (cm)	Weight (kg)
178	80
157	57
182	81
155	53
148	42
175	74

  These results are presented on the scatter graph below.

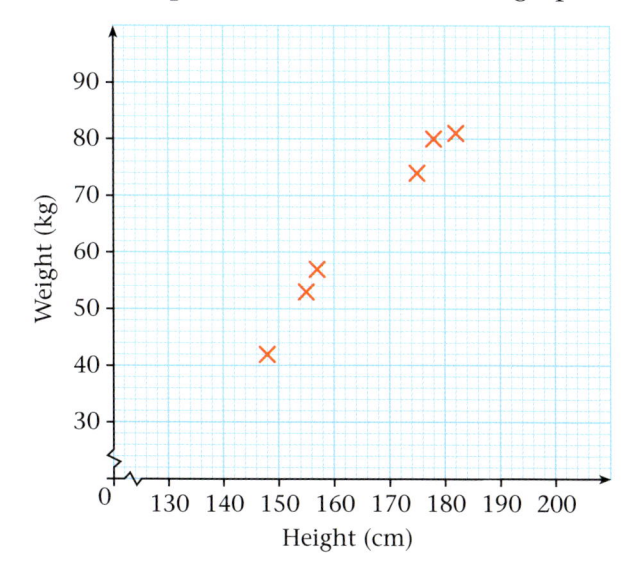

The results for a further four people are:

Height (cm)	192	138	163	180
Weight (kg)	88	36	60	79

(a) Plot these extra four values on a copy of the scatter graph.
(b) Describe the relationship between the heights and weights of these ten people.
(c) Draw a line of best fit on your scatter graph.
(d) Use your line of best fit to estimate
   (i) the likely weight of a person of height 150 cm
   (ii) the likely height of a person who weighs 72 kg.

5.2 Time series

- A **time series graph** is a line graph that shows data collected at timed intervals (e.g. hourly, daily, weekly, …).

Example 2

The table below shows information about the average midday temperatures in Rhodes during the summer months.

Month	April	May	June	July	Aug	Sept	Oct
Temperature (°C)	18	21	26	29	31	27	23

(a) Draw a time series graph for this data.

During the same summer months, the average midday temperatures in the UK are:

Month	April	May	June	July	Aug	Sept	Oct
Temperature (°C)	13	18	20	22	22	19	14

(b) Draw a time series graph for this data on the same axes as for the Rhodes data.
(c) During which of these summer months is
   (i) the average midday temperature in Rhodes highest
   (ii) the average midday temperature in the UK lowest
   (iii) the smallest difference between the average midday temperatures in Rhodes and the UK
   (iv) the greatest difference between the average midday temperatures in Rhodes and the UK?

Mrs Jones wants to go on holiday to Rhodes when the average midday temperature is not above 30 °C. She wants to go when the difference between the average midday temperatures in Rhodes and the UK is as high as possible.

(d) During which month should Mrs Jones go to Rhodes?

(a) (b)

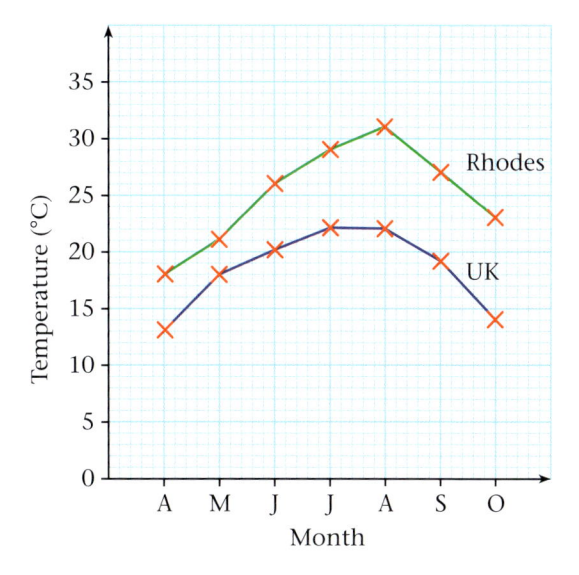

(c) (i) The average midday temperature in Rhodes is highest in August.
(ii) The average midday temperature in the UK is lowest in April.
(iii) The smallest difference between the midday temperatures in Rhodes and the UK is in May.
(iv) The greatest difference between the midday temperatures in Rhodes and the UK is in August and October.

(d) October

All these answers are read from the graph.

Months when temperature in Rhodes is not above 30 °C are April, May, June, July, September, October. Of these, the greatest difference between UK and Rhodes temperature is in October.

Example 3

As part of a project, Gemma has gathered information about the quarterly gas bill at her home over a period of four years.
The information is given in the table on page 56.

Date of bill	Amount
Feb 2002	£255
May 2002	£204
Aug 2002	£112
Nov 2002	£156

Date of bill	Amount
Feb 2003	£263
May 2003	£210
Aug 2003	£117
Nov 2003	£160

Date of bill	Amount
Feb 2004	£270
May 2004	£212
Aug 2004	£120
Nov 2004	£172

Date of bill	Amount
Feb 2005	£294
May 2005	£223
Aug 2005	£128
Nov 2005	£185

Represent this information as a time series.

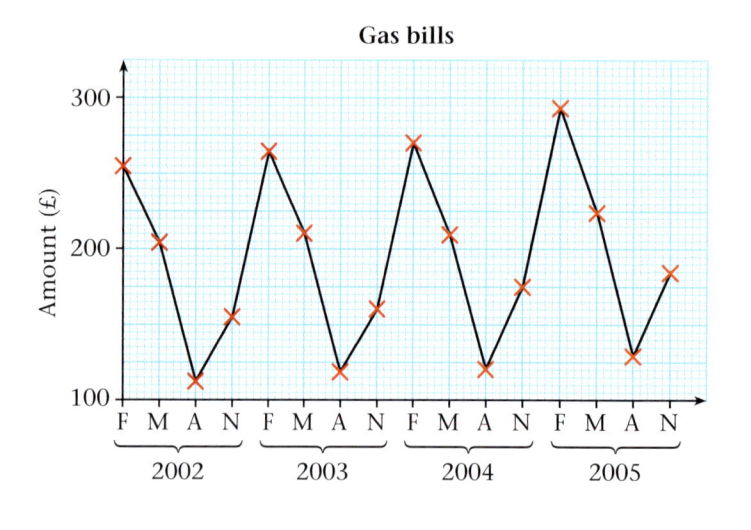

The time series graph shows seasonal variations. The bills are higher in the winter months, when more gas is used.

Activity – Fishing in the North Sea

This time series graph shows the effect of fishing on the numbers of cod in the North Sea.

Explain what the time series graph shows.

Investigate the effect of fishing on other types of fish.

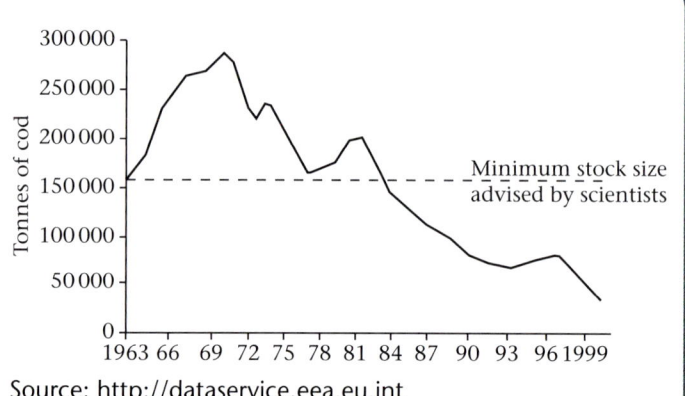

Source: http://dataservice.eea.eu.int

Exercise 5B

1. The table gives the average midday temperatures in the Costa del Sol and the UK during the winter months. All temperatures are in °C.

Month	Oct	Nov	Dec	Jan	Feb	Mar	Apr
Costa del Sol	24	19	17	16	17	18	21
UK	14	13	7	6	7	10	13

   (a) On the same axes, draw a time series graph for each set of data.
   (b) Which month has the smallest difference in average midday temperatures in the UK and the Costa del Sol?
   (c) Work out the difference between the **means** of the average midday temperatures in the UK and the Costa del Sol during these months.

2. Wendy bought a beach hut in July 1992 for £34 000. The table shows its value in £1000s, for the next 13 years.

Year	92	93	94	95	96	97	98	99	00	01	02	03	04	05
Value	34	37	40	33	31	31	32	33	34	38	40	44	53	64

   (a) Plot this data as points in a time series. Draw a time series graph for this data.
   (b) Write *four* comments about how the value of Wendy's beach hut varied between 1992 and 2005.

3. The table shows information about Mrs Howe's gas bill, in £s, for the years from 2001 to 2005.

Year	1st quarter	2nd quarter	3rd quarter	4th quarter
2001	312	264	142	182
2002	325	271	150	190
2003	340	280	155	201
2004	346	288	172	218
2005	355	298	180	230

   Represent this information graphically as a time series.

4 Joseph works as a salesman. His quarterly sales figures, in £1000, for the years from 2001 to 2005 are given below.

	2001	2002	2003	2004	2005
Jan	110	115	118	123	139
April	152	158	162	167	174
July	252	260	263	268	273
Oct	207	210	215	221	229

Represent this information as a time series.

5.3 Retail Prices Index

- The **Retail Prices Index** (RPI) measures the change in the prices of goods and services.

The government collects data on the cost of items each month, to update the RPI.

Example 4

Workwell is a small company. It keeps its wages in line with changes in the Retail Prices Index (RPI).

Sam joined Workwell on 1 January 1987.
His weekly wage then was exactly £200 and the RPI was 100.
For the next 19 years he stayed at Workwell doing the same job.
Work out what Sam's weekly wage would have been
(a) during January 1997, when the RPI was 154.4
(b) during January 2006, when the RPI was 193.4.

(a) In January 1987, the RPI was 100.
   In January 1997, the RPI was 154.4.
   So the proportional change (or factor) in the RPI
   $= \frac{154.4}{100} = 1.544$.
   So to keep in line with changes in the RPI, Sam's weekly wage in January 1997 was
      wage in January 1987 × proportional change in RPI
      = £200 × 1.544 = £308.80.

(b) In January 2006, the RPI was 193.4.
   So the proportional change in RPI between January 1987 and January 2001 was $\frac{193.4}{100} = 1.934$.
   So to keep in line with changes in the RPI, Sam's weekly wage in January 2006 was
      £200 × 1.934 = £386.80.

Example 5

The table shows the Retail Prices Index in the UK and in Malta from January 1995 to January 2001.

Year	1995	1996	1997	1998	1999	2000	2001
(RPI) (UK)	146.0	150.2	154.4	159.5	163.4	166.6	171.1
(RPI) (Malta)	100	99.87	103.57	107.10	108.62	112.24	112.95

(a) Plot the RPI in Malta against the RPI in the UK as points on a scatter diagram.

(b) On your scatter diagram draw the line of best fit.

(c) Comment on the correlation between the RPI in Malta and the RPI in the UK.

The local newspaper in Malta claimed that price rises on the island between 1995 and 2001 had been lower than prices rises in the UK over the same period.

(d) Comment on the newspaper's claim.

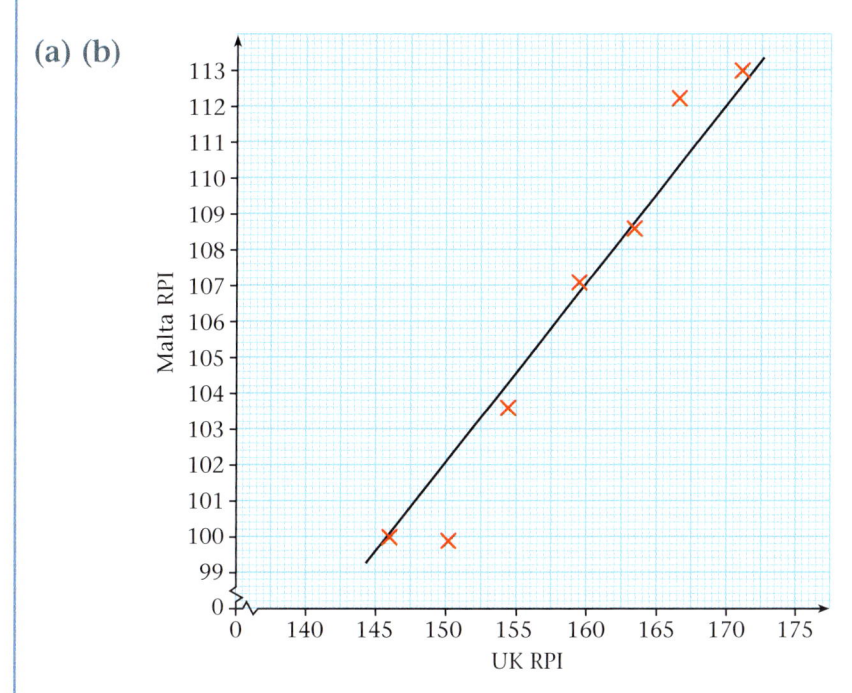

(a) (b)

[Scatter diagram: Malta RPI vs UK RPI, showing points from (146, 100) to (171, 113) with line of best fit]

(c) The scatter diagram shows **positive correlation** between the RPI in the UK and the RPI in Malta.

> As the RPI increased in the UK, it also increased in Malta.

(d) Between 1995 and 2001 the proportional changes in RPI were

For UK: $\dfrac{171.1}{140.0} = 1.1719$ For Malta: $\dfrac{112.95}{100} = 1.1295$

The change in RPI for the UK is greater than the change in RPI for Malta over the period from 1995 to 2001.
The newspaper's claim is correct.

Chapter 5 Scatter graphs, correlation and time series

Example 6

In January 2000 the RPI was 166.6.
A newspaper cost 65p in January 2000.
In January 2006 the RPI was 193.4.

(a) Use the RPI to work out the cost of a newspaper in January 2006.
(b) What assumptions did you make?

(a) January 2000 RPI = 166.6
January 2006 RPI = 193.4

Proportional change = $\dfrac{193.4}{166.6}$

Cost of newspaper in 2006 = $\dfrac{193.4}{166.6} \times 65$p

= 75.45…p

= 75p

Round the answer to the nearest penny.

(b) The assumption was that the price of the newspaper increased in line with the RPI.

Exercise 5C

1. Asif joined Wellworkers Ltd in August 1996 at a salary of £12 500 per year.
The RPI in August 1996 was 153.1.
In August 2005 the RPI was 192.6.
Between August 1996 and August 2005, Asif's salary increased in line with the RPI.
Work out Asif's salary in August 2005.

2. In January 1975 the RPI was 30.39.
In January 2006 the RPI was 193.4.
In January 1975 the price of a loaf of bread was 12p.
Assuming that bread prices follow the changes in the RPI, work out the price of a similar loaf of bread in January 2006.

3. In December 2005 the RPI was 194.1.
In December 1960 the RPI was 12.62.
The price of a loaf of bread was 68p in December 2005.
Stating your assumptions, work out an estimate of the price of a similar loaf of bread in December 1960.

4 The table below provides information about the Retail Prices Index in the UK and on the island of Guernsey during the months of September from 1994 to 2001.

	1994	1995	1996	1997	1998	1999	2000	2001
UK	145.0	150.6	153.8	159.3	164.4	166.2	171.7	174.6
Guernsey	100.2	104.2	106.2	110.9	115.4	117.4	122.7	125.9

(a) Plot the two sets of data as points on a scatter graph.
(b) Draw the line of best fit on the scatter graph.
(c) Comment on the relationship between the RPI in the UK and the RPI on Guernsey.

A local radio station on Guernsey claims that during the years from 1994 to 2001 the price rises on the island have been lower than those on the mainland UK.

(d) Explain whether the table of RPIs provides evidence to support this claim or not.

Mixed exercise 5

1 Students' mark in a Mathematics examination and an English examination were as follows.

Mathematics	25	38	43	68	80	74	55	29	47	59	61
English	31	37	46	65	77	76	58	32	52	56	65

(a) Draw a scatter graph to represent this data.
(b) Comment on the relationship between the marks in the two subjects.
(c) Draw the line of best fit on your scatter graph.

A student took the Mathematics examination and scored a mark of 50.
The same student was ill on the day of the English examination and did not take it.

(d) Use the line of best fit to estimate a mark for this student in the English examination.
(e) Represent
   (i) the Mathematics marks
   (ii) the English marks
   on a stem and leaf diagram.

2 The table shows the hours of sunshine and the snowfall, in mm, in ten towns during last winter.

Sunshine (hours)	450	255	360	230	420	200	440	175	320	420
Snowfall (mm)	20	40	30	58	48	56	28	60	50	40

The points for the first six results in the table have been plotted in a scatter graph:

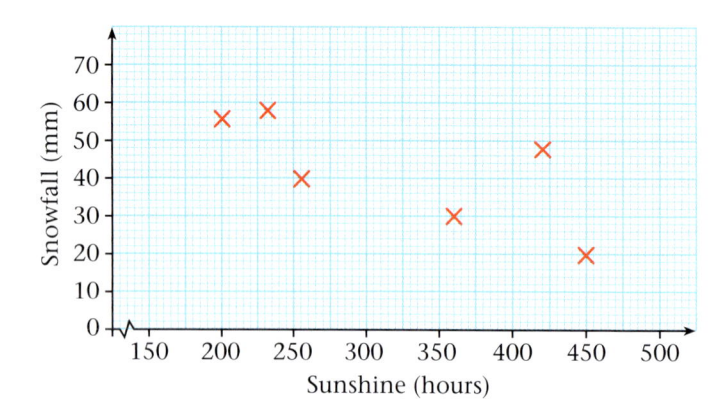

(a) Copy the scatter graph and plot the other four points.

(b) Describe the correlation between the hours of sunshine and the snowfall.

(c) Draw the line of best fit on your scatter graph.

(d) Represent the snowfall on a stem and leaf diagram.

3 The diagrams represent three scatter graphs:

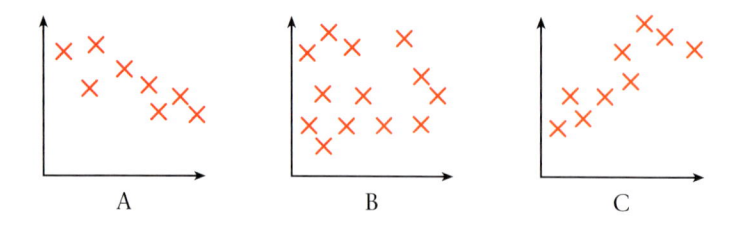

A   B   C

Use one of the following words to describe the correlation shown in each graph:

    Positive   Negative   None

4 The scatter graph shows the Science mark and the Maths mark for 15 students.

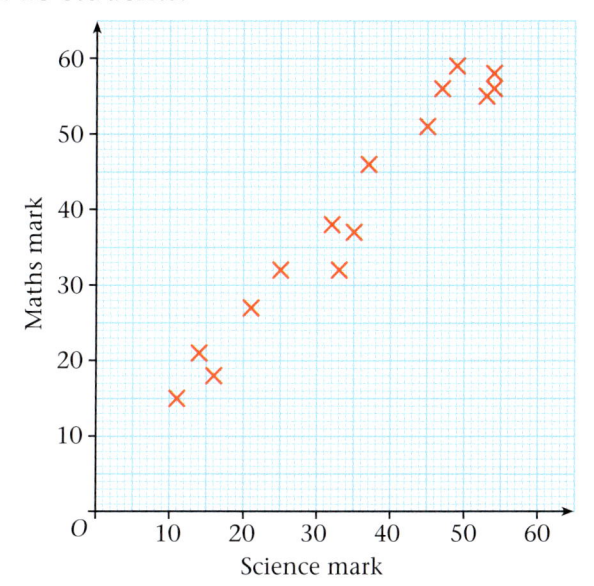

(a) What type of correlation does this scatter graph show?
(b) Copy the scatter graph. Draw the line of best fit.

Sophie's science mark was 42.

(c) Use your line of best fit to estimate Sophie's Maths mark. [E]

5 The scatter graph shows information about the value of a house and the area of floor space in the house.

Comment on this information.

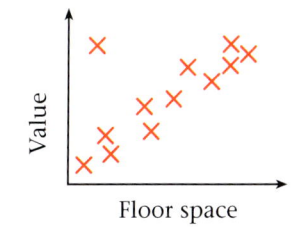

6 Mrs Sharma pays her gas bill in March, June, August and December each year.
The table below provides information about her gas bills for the years 2003 to 2005.

	March	June	August	December
2003	£268	£182	£121	£206
2004	£284	£191	£128	£217
2005	£301	£199	£140	£230

(a) Represent this information on a time series graph.
(b) Make three comments about how Mrs Sharma's gas bill varied from March 2003 to December 2005.

7 The government's estimate of the population of England in mid-2000 was 49 997 100.
It was estimated that the distribution of this population by region was:

English region	Population estimate
North East	2 577 300
North West	6 893 900
Yorkshire and Humber	5 057 900
East Midlands	4 207 900
West Midlands	5 335 400
East Anglia	5 459 600
London	7 375 100
South East	8 114 900
South West	4 975 100

(a) Represent this data on a bar chart.
(b) Represent this data on a pie chart.
(c) Which is the **modal** region?

The average price of a house in each of these English regions in the year 2000 is given in the table below.

(d) Write these average prices in order, starting with the smallest.
(e) Draw a scatter graph for the average price of a house against the population.
(f) Draw a line of best fit on your scatter graph.
(g) Comment on the relationship between house prices and population.

English region	Average house price
North East	£52 500
North West	£65 000
Yorkshire and Humber	£61 000
East Midlands	£68 850
West Midlands	£76 200
East Anglia	£82 500
London	£147 500
South East	£120 000
South West	£88 800

8 The quarterly figures (in 1000s) for the number of people visiting a theme park for the years 2002 to 2005 are given below.

Quarter	2002	2003	2004	2005
1st	112	113	102	124
2nd	206	204	185	223
3rd	517	510	470	540
4th	380	320	290	395

(a) Represent this information as a time series graph.
(b) Comment on any seasonal patterns in the data.

Summary of key points

1 A linear relationship between two sets of data is called a **correlation**.

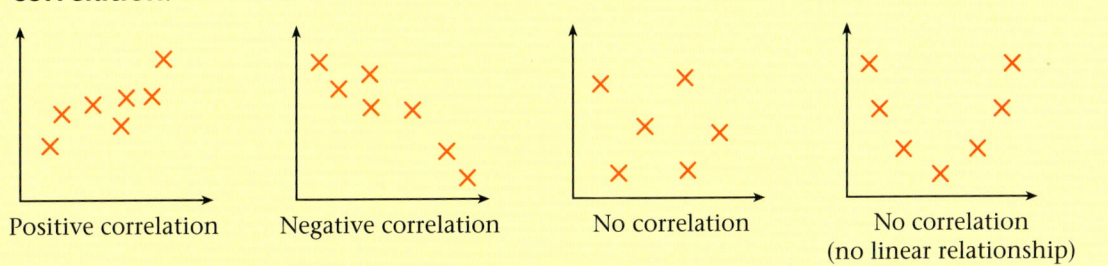

Positive correlation   Negative correlation   No correlation   No correlation (no linear relationship)

2 The **line of best fit** is a straight line that passes through or is as close to as many of the plotted points as possible.

3 A line of best fit gives a model for how two variables are related. The closer the plotted points are to the line the better the correlation.

4 A line of best fit can be used to estimate other data values.

5 A **time series graph** is a line graph that shows data collected at timed intervals (e.g. hourly, daily, weekly, …).

6 The **Retail Prices Index** (RPI) measures the change in the prices of goods and services.

6 Probability

6.1 Probability scales

- An event that is *certain* to happen has a **probability of 1**.
- An event that *cannot happen* has a **probability of 0**.
- The probability that an event will happen is always greater than or equal to 0 (impossible) and less than or equal to 1 (certain).
  This can be written:
  $0 \leqslant \text{probability} \leqslant 1$

Example 1

Here is a probability scale labelled in words.

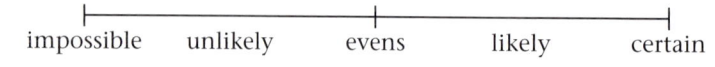

| impossible | unlikely | evens | likely | certain |

On the scale mark the probability that
(a) it will snow in London on 1 August (use the letter A)
(b) the day before Christmas Day will be Christmas Eve (use the letter B)
(c) the bottom card of a well-shuffled pack of cards will be a black card (use the letter C)
(d) there will be at least one rainy day during March (use the letter D)
(e) ice cream will not melt if you put it in a hot oven for half an hour (use the letter E).

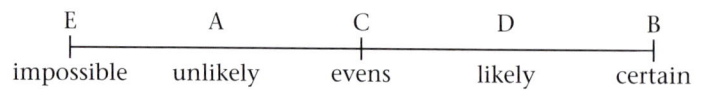

| E | A | C | D | B |
| impossible | unlikely | evens | likely | certain |

Example 2

Here is a probability scale.

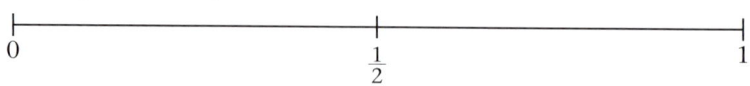

$0 \quad\quad\quad \frac{1}{2} \quad\quad\quad 1$

On the scale mark the probability that
(a) the next baby to be born will be female (use the letter F)
(b) the day immediately following Christmas Day will be Boxing Day (use the letter B)

(c) the next thing you see flying in the sky will be a pink elephant (use the letter E).

(a) We know that about half of newborn babies are boys and about half are girls. So the probability of the baby being a girl is about $\frac{1}{2}$.

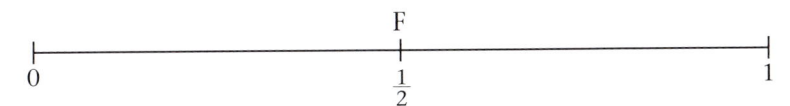

```
          F
|---------+---------|
0         1/2       1
```

(b) It is a certainty that Christmas Day will be followed by Boxing Day, so the probability = 1.

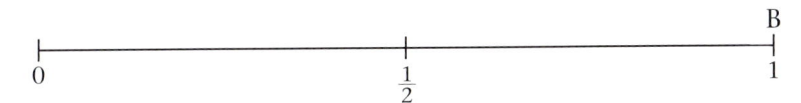

```
                              B
|---------+---------|
0         1/2       1
```

(c) We know that elephants cannot fly and neither are they pink. So it is impossible for you to see a flying pink elephant. So this probability = 0.

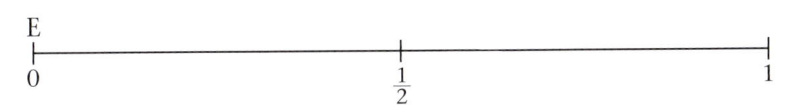

```
E
|---------+---------|
0         1/2       1
```

- If all the possible outcomes of an event are equally likely, the probability that the event will happen is

$$\text{probability} = \frac{\text{number of successful outcomes}}{\text{total number of possible outcomes}}$$

Example 3

On a probability scale, mark the probability that
(a) the top card on a well-shuffled pack of cards will be red
(b) the bottom card on a well-shuffled pack of cards will be a Heart
(c) when an ordinary dice is thrown it lands showing 5.

(a) Half of the cards in a pack are red.
So the probability that the top card is red is $\frac{1}{2}$.

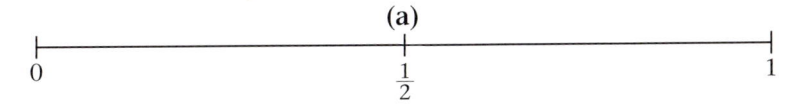

```
              (a)
|---------+---------|
0         1/2       1
```

Each card is equally likely to end up on the top of the pack.

(b) There are 52 cards in a pack. 13 of them are Hearts.

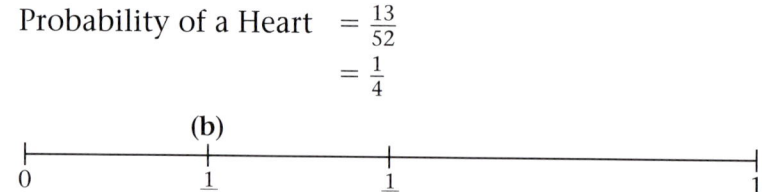

Probability of a Heart $= \frac{13}{52}$
$= \frac{1}{4}$

13 successful outcomes
52 possible outcomes

(c) Probability of a 5 $= \frac{1}{6}$

1 successful outcome (the score 5)
6 possible outcomes

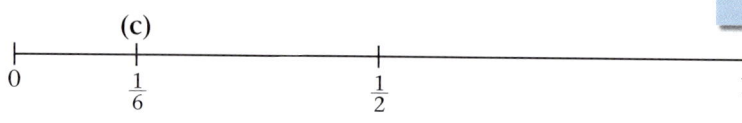

Exercise 6A

1 Copy this probability scale.

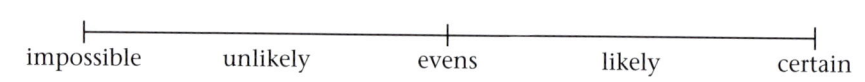

impossible   unlikely   evens   likely   certain

(a) Mark with T the likelihood of a fair coin landing tails when it is thrown once.
(b) Mark with C the likelihood of the day before Boxing Day being Christmas Day.
(c) Mark with S the likelihood of the sun shining in London on at least one day next July.
(d) Mark with D the likelihood that a dinosaur will walk down the main road tomorrow.
(e) Mark with J the likelihood that Mr Jones will cut his lawn at a time when it is pouring down with rain.

2 Copy this probability scale.

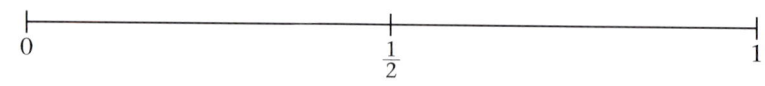

(a) Mark with T the probability of getting a tail when a fair coin is thrown.
(b) Mark with S the probability of getting a 9 when a fair six-sided dice is thrown.
(c) Mark with N the probability of getting a number less than 100 when a fair six-sided dice is thrown.

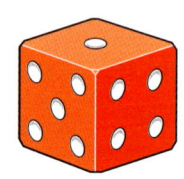

3 Three letters are marked on this probability scale.

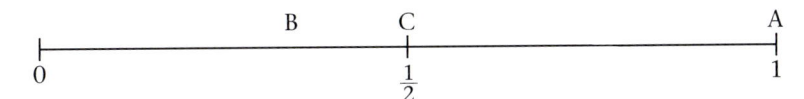

Match the letters to these probabilities:
(a) the probability that a fair six-sided dice will land with its top face showing a number less than 3
(b) the probability that the sun will set tomorrow
(c) the probability that when it is thrown once a fair coin will land heads.

4 Copy this probability scale.

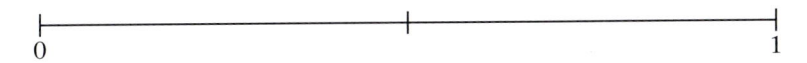

Mark
(a) with the letter S, the probability that it will snow in London in June.
(b) with the letter H, the probability that when a fair coin is thrown once it comes down heads.
(c) with the letter M, the probability that it will rain in Manchester next year. [E]

6.2 Mutually exclusive outcomes

- Outcomes are **mutually exclusive** when they cannot happen at the same time.

Example 4

This five-sided spinner is in the shape of a regular pentagon. Each section of the spinner is labelled with a letter.
The spinner is spun once.
Write down the probability that it will land on
(a) the section labelled R
(b) a section labelled U
(c) a section labelled Z
(d) a section labelled with a letter of the alphabet
(e) a section labelled with a letter that is **not** a vowel
(f) a section labelled either U or R.

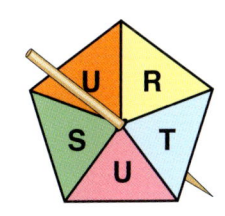

(a) The spinner could land on any one of five sections. But of these only one is labelled R. So the probability of it landing on this section is $\frac{1}{5}$.

Instead of writing 'probability of R' you can write P(R).

(b) Of the five sections, two are labelled U, so P(U) = $\frac{2}{5}$.

(c) There are no sections labelled Z, so landing on one is impossible. Therefore P(Z) = 0.

(d) Each and every section is labelled with a letter. So it is a certainty that the spinner must land on a section labelled with a letter. So this probability = 1.

(e) The only vowel on the spinner is U. There are three sections with letters that are **not** vowels. So the probability of landing on a section with a letter that is not a vowel is $\frac{3}{5}$.

(f) There are two sections labelled U and one section labelled R. So there are three sections altogether labelled U or R. So the probability of landing on a section labelled either U or R is P(U or R) = P(U) + P(R) = $\frac{2}{5} + \frac{1}{5} = \frac{3}{5}$.

Example 5

A four-sided dice labelled 1, 2, 3, 4 is thrown once. What is the probability that the score is

(a) an even number (b) an odd number (c) a number less than 4?

(a) P(even number) = P(2) + P(4)
$= \frac{1}{4} + \frac{1}{4} = \frac{1}{2}$

There are four equally likely outcomes: 1, 2, 3, 4.

(b) P(odd number) = P(1) + P(3)
$= \frac{1}{4} + \frac{1}{4} = \frac{1}{2}$

P(even number) = P(2 or 4) = P(2) + P(4).

(c) P(a number less than 4) = P(1) + P(2) + P(3)
$= \frac{1}{4} + \frac{1}{4} + \frac{1}{4}$
$= \frac{3}{4}$

The scores less than 4 are 1, 2 and 3.

Exercise 6B

1 Joan has three equal-sized coloured balls in a bag. One ball is red, one ball is blue and the other ball is green. She chooses a ball at random.
Write down the probability that
(a) the ball she chooses will be blue
(b) the ball she chooses will be yellow.

2 The faces of a six-sided dice are labelled 1 to 6.
   The dice is rolled once.
   Write down the probability that its upper face shows
   (a) 4
   (b) a number greater than 3
   (c) an even number
   (b) a number greater between 7 and 10.

3 Farouk has a box of 15 chocolates.
   Eight are plain, six are milk and one is white.
   He chooses a chocolate at random.
   (a) Write down the probability that the chocolate chosen is white.
   (b) Write down the probability of Farouk choosing a fruit gum.
   (c) Write down the probability that the chocolate chosen is milk.
   (d) Write down the probability that the chocolate chosen is either plain or white.

4 The diagram shows a six-sided fair spinner.
   The spinner is in the shape of a regular hexagon.
   The sections of the spinner are labelled with the letters A, B, C, D and E.
   The spinner is to be spun once. Write down the probability
   (a) that it will land on D
   (b) that it will land on A
   (c) that it will land on a vowel
   (d) that it will land on P.

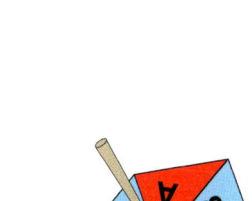

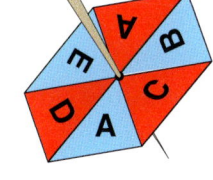

6.3 Listing outcomes

○ 23 Combined events animation

Example 6

Each section of this square spinner is labelled with a number.
The coin has two faces – heads and tails.
The spinner is to be spun once.
The coin is to be thrown once.
One possible joint outcome of the two events is (1, heads)
(a) List all the possible joint outcomes of the two events.
(b) Explain why the probability of the spinner landing on 1 and the coin landing heads is $\frac{1}{8}$.

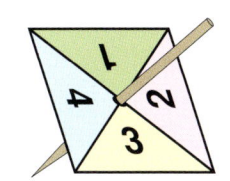

(a) (1, heads) (1, tails)
    (2, heads) (2, tails)
    (3, heads) (3, tails)
    (4, heads) (4, tails)

> List all the outcomes systematically.

(b) There are 8 possible outcomes.
    Each of these outcomes is equally likely.
    The outcome (1, heads) is one of these outcomes.
    So the probability of this outcome is $\frac{1}{8}$.

> The 8 possible outcomes are listed in part (a).

- A **sample space diagram** shows all possible outcomes of one or more events.

Example 7

The diagram represents a fair coin and a fair spinner.
The spinner is in the shape of an equilateral triangle.
Asif throws the coin once and spins the spinner once.

(a) Construct a sample space diagram to show all the possible outcomes.
(b) Work out the probability of the joint outcome heads and a number less than 3.

(a) The sample space diagram is:

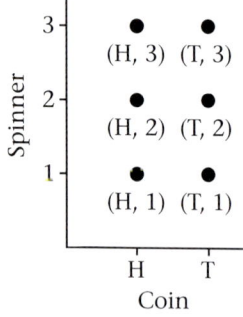

```
Spinner
  3      •        •
        (H, 3)  (T, 3)
  2      •        •
        (H, 2)  (T, 2)
  1      •        •
        (H, 1)  (T, 1)
         H        T
             Coin
```

(b) For the joint outcome of heads and a number less than 3, the 'successful' outcomes are

(H, 1)   (H, 2)

> Two successful outcomes.

From the sample space diagram, there are six joint outcomes in total.
So probability (H and number < 3) = $\frac{2}{6} = \frac{1}{3}$

Exercise 6C

1 Tamsin has four places to visit:

London, Manchester, Bristol and Edinburgh.

In each case she has three possible methods of travel:
car, bus or train.

One possible journey she could make is

London by train.

List all the possible journeys Tamsin could make.

2 This fair spinner is to be spun once and the dice rolled once.

One possible outcome could be (A, 1).

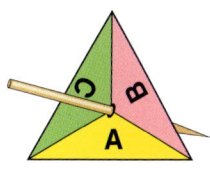

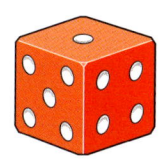

(a) Draw a sample space diagram to show the possible joint outcomes.

(b) Write down the probability of the joint outcome (A, 1).

(c) Write down the probability of the joint outcome (D, 3).

A on the spinner
1 on the dice

3 A game is played with two fair spinners. The spinners are spun at the same time.

The diagram below shows the result (red, 3).

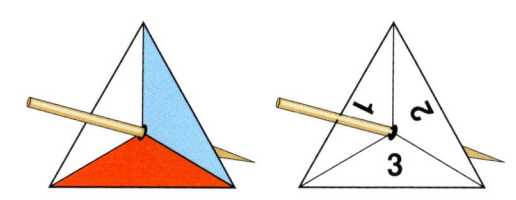

(a) Draw a sample space diagram to show all the possible results when the spinners are spun once.

(b) Use your list to work out the probability of (blue, 1) when the spinners are spun once.

4 Kylie has a fair coin and a fair six-sided dice.
She throws the coin once.
She rolls the dice once.
The diagram shows the outcomes (head, 3).

(a) Draw a sample space diagram to show all the possible outcomes when the coin is thrown once and the dice is rolled once.

(b) Work out the probability of (tail, 6).

5 The diagram shows two fair spinners.
   Each spinner is spun once and the joint outcomes recorded. 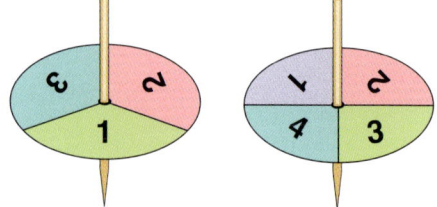
   (a) Draw a sample space diagram for the joint outcomes.
   (b) Find the probability of the joint outcome first spinner stops on 3 and second spinner stops on 4.
   The numbers on the two sections that the spinners land on are added to give a total score.
   (c) Work out the probability of obtaining a total score
       (i)   of 4
       (ii) which is an even number
       (iii) which is an odd number.

6.4 Probability of an event not happening

- The probabilities of all the mutually exclusive outcomes of an event add to 1.
- The probabilities of an event **not** happening
  = 1 − probability of the event happening.
  P(not A) = 1 − P(A)

'Event happens' and 'event does not happen' are mutually exclusive. So P(happens) + P(does not happen) = 1

Example 8

Jack has a box of chocolates.
Twelve are plain, five are milk and three are white.
Jack takes a chocolate at random.
What is the probability that the chocolate is
(a) milk
(b) not plain
(c) a caramel?

'At random' means every chocolate is equally likely to be chosen.

(a) There are 20 chocolates. 5 are milk.
    P(milk) = $\frac{5}{20}$ = $\frac{1}{4}$

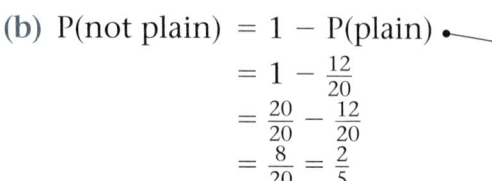

(b) P(not plain) = 1 − P(plain)
    = 1 − $\frac{12}{20}$
    = $\frac{20}{20}$ − $\frac{12}{20}$
    = $\frac{8}{20}$ = $\frac{2}{5}$

(c) There are no caramels in the box, so
    P(caramel) = 0

You can simplify the fraction but you don't **need** to unless the question asks you to.

20 chocolates; 12 plain
P(plain) = $\frac{12}{20}$

- You can write probabilities as fractions, decimals or percentages.

Example 9

The probability of a new light bulb being faulty is 0.002. Work out the probability of a new light bulb *not* being faulty.

Probability of not being faulty = 1 − probability of being faulty
= 1 − 0.002
= 0.998

Example 10

The diagram represents a spinner in the shape of a pentagon. The spinner is biased.

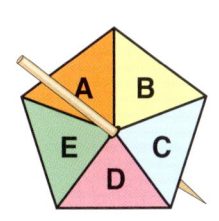

When it is spun once, the probability of it stopping on each of the sections A, B, C and D is shown in the table below.

Section	A	B	C	D	E
Probability	0.23	0.18	0.16	0.22	

The spinner is spun once.
(a) Work out the probability that it stops on section E.
(b) Work out the probability of it *not* stopping on section A.

(a) The sum of the probabilities = 1
So 0.23 + 0.18 + 0.16 + 0.22 + P(E) = 1
0.79 + P(E) = 1
P(E) = 1 − 0.79 = 0.21
So probability of stopping on E = 0.21

(b) Probability of not A = 1 − probability of A
= 1 − 0.23
= 0.77

> It is certain that the spinner will land on A or B or C or D or E, so the sum of the probabilities = 1.

Exercise 6D

1. The probability of a newly laid egg being cracked is 0.03. Work out the probability of a newly laid egg *not* being cracked.

2. The probability of a train being late is 23%. Work out the probability of the train *not* being late.

3. Debbie has a bag which contains ten equal-sized coloured counters.
   Six of the counters are red, three are blue and one is white.
   She selects a counter at random from the bag.
   Work out the probability that the selected counter is
   (a) blue
   (b) not white
   (c) either red or white
   (d) green.

4. A dice has faces numbered, 1, 2, 3, 4, 5 and 6.
   The dice is biased.
   Some of the probabilities of it landing with each face uppermost when it is rolled once are shown in the table below.

Face	1	2	3	4	5	6
Probability	0.20	0.11	0.17	0.19	0.21	

   The dice is to be rolled once.
   Work out the probability of it landing with 6 on the uppermost face.

5. A train can be either **early**, **late** or **on time**.
   The probability of the train being early is 0.07.
   The probability of the train being late is 0.24.
   Work out the probability of the train being on time.

6. Imran has a box of 25 felt-tip pens.
   Twelve of the pens are red.
   Eight of the pens are blue.
   The rest of the pens are black.
   Imran chooses one pen at random from the box.
   What is the probability that Imran will choose
   (a) a red pen
   (b) a black pen
   (c) a pen that is not blue?

6.5 Estimating likely outcomes

Example 11

On Sarita's MP3 player, 30% of the tracks are indie, 50% are hip hop and 20% are pop.
Sarita sets the player to 'shuffle', so it selects and plays tracks at random.
(a) What type of track is it most likely to play?
(b) What type of track is it least likely to play?
Write down the probability that the first track played is
(c) not pop
(d) folk.

(a) It is most likely to play hip hop, as this has the highest percentage of tracks.
(b) It is least likely to play pop, as this has the lowest percentage of tracks.
(c) P(pop) = 20%
So P(not pop) = 100% − P(pop)
= 100% − 20%
= 80%

> P(not pop) = 1 − P(pop)
> 100% = 1

(d) There is no folk on the MP3 player, so
P(folk) = 0

Example 12

The probability of a new computer being faulty is 0.002.
(a) Work out the probability of a new computer *not* being faulty.
A computer superstore has 12 000 new computers in stock.
(b) Work out an estimate of the number of these new computers likely to be faulty.

(a) Probability (not faulty) = 1 − probability (faulty)
= 1 − 0.002
= 0.998
(b) Probability of being faulty is 0.002 (i.e. 2 out of every 1000 will be faulty).
So the likely number of faulty computers out of a batch of 12 000 is
0.002 × 12 000 = 24

> 0.002 = 2 thousandths
> = $\frac{2}{1000}$

Exercise 6E

1. A bag contains 20 coloured snooker balls.
   Nine of the balls are red, six are blue, three are white and two are black.
   A ball is to be selected at random from the bag.
   (a) Which colour is the ball selected least likely to be? Give your reasoning.
   (b) Write down the probability of the selected ball being blue.
   (c) Work out the probability of the selected ball being
      (i) blue or black   (ii) red, white or black
      (iii) not red   (iv) green.

2. The probability of a newly laid egg being cracked is 0.004.
   (a) Work out the probability of a newly laid egg *not* being cracked.

   A supermarket took delivery of 140 000 newly laid eggs.
   (b) Work out, showing all of your reasoning, the most likely number of eggs out of the 140 000 to be cracked.

3. The probability of a train being late is $\frac{1}{15}$.
   Work out the probability of the train *not* being late.

4. The probability of the school bus being late is estimated to be 15%. During the year the school bus makes 195 journeys to the school.
   Work out an estimate for the most likely number of times the school bus will be late during the year.

5. James write books. The probability of him spelling a word incorrectly is 0.003.
   James's last book contained 120 000 words. Work out an estimate of the most likely number of words in this book to be spelled incorrectly.

6.6 Estimating probability

- The **relative frequency** of an outcome in an experiment is
  $$\text{relative frequency} = \frac{\text{number of successful trials}}{\text{total number of trials}}$$
- For a trial or experiment the **estimated probability** is given by the relative frequency.

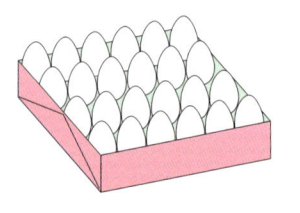

Example 13

The four candidates standing at the local election are

Anderson, Barnes, Clarke and **Deyhna**.

Shortly before the election, a market research company ask a random sample of 1000 voters the question.

Which candidate do you intend to vote for?

The responses are:

Name	Anderson	Barnes	Clarke	Deyhna
Number of voters	125	462	285	128

A voter is selected at random.
Using the information in the table, work out the best estimate for
(a) the probability of this voter voting for Clarke
(b) the probability of this voter *not* voting for Barnes.

(a) The best estimate for

$$P(\text{Clarke}) = \frac{\text{number saying they will vote for Clarke}}{\text{total number of people asked}}$$

$$= \frac{285}{1000}$$

$$= 0.285$$

(b) The best estimate for
$$P(\text{not Barnes}) = 1 - P(\text{Barnes})$$
$$= 1 - \frac{462}{1000}$$
$$= 1 - 0.462$$
$$= 0.538$$

Example 14

The diagram represents a spinner.
It is thought that the spinner is biased.
Chantal spins the spinner 100 times and records the letter it stops on.
Her results are:

Letter	A	B	C
Frequency	28	30	42

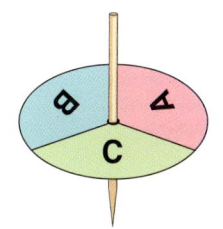

Zoë then spins the spinner 100 times and records the letter it stops on.

Her results are:

Letter	A	B	C
Frequency	26	36	38

(a) Explain why there is a difference between the two sets of results.

(b) Use the information to work out the *best* estimates for the probability of the spinner stopping on each of the three letters.

(c) Explain whether or not the spinner appears to be biased.

(a) The results of spinning the spinner are random, so it is very unlikely that two sets of spins will give exactly the same results.

(b) Combining Chantal's and Zoë's results gives:

Letter	A	B	C
Frequency	28 + 26 = 54	30 + 36 = 66	42 + 38 = 80

> Increasing the number of trials gives a more accurate result. For the *best* estimate, combine the results.

The best estimates are

$P(A) = \frac{54}{200} = 0.27$

$P(B) = \frac{66}{200} = 0.33$

$P(C) = \frac{80}{200} = 0.40$

(c) For an unbiased spinner the probabilities of stopping on A, B and C would be

A	B	C
$\frac{1}{3} = 0.3\dot{3}$	$\frac{1}{3} = 0.3\dot{3}$	$\frac{1}{3} = 0.3\dot{3}$

> This is the **theoretical probability** – what should happen 'in theory'.

We cannot be certain, but the estimated probabilities of

A	B	C
0.27	0.33	0.40

based on 200 trials, suggest that the spinner is biased.

> To see if a spinner is fair, you compare its experimental results with the theoretical probability.

Activity – Drawing pin

Throw a drawing pin 10 times and count the number of times it lands point up.

Repeat for more sets of 10 throws, up to 100 throws in total.

Copy and complete the table.

Number of throws	Number of times drawing pin lands point up	Relative frequency
10		
20		
…		
…		
100		

Draw a graph to show estimated probability for different numbers of throws.

Comment on your results.

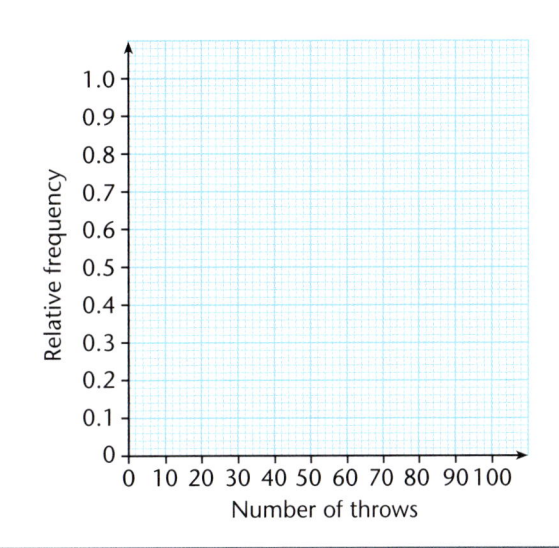

Exercise 6F

1 A market research company conducts a survey into students' travel to school. They choose a random sample of 2000 students from all types of school across the country.
   The results of the survey are:

Method of travel	Walk	Car	Train	Cycle	Bus
Frequency	758	352	206	103	581

(a) Work out the best estimates for the probability that a student chosen at random will normally
   (i)   travel to school by bus
   (ii) travel to school by car
   (iii) *not* walk to school.
(b) Explain what the market research company will need to do to improve on these estimates.

2 The diagram represents a spinner.
   The spinner is thought to be biased.
   John spins the spinner 100 times and records the letter it
   stops on each time.
   His results are:

Section	A	B	C	D
Frequency	12	42	17	29

   Mandy spins the spinner 300 times.
   Her results are:

Section	A	B	C	D
Frequency	41	129	58	72

   Mandy spins the spinner three times as many as John.
   (a) Explain why the frequencies in Mandy's table are not
       three times those in John's table.
   (b) Use the results to work out the best estimate for the
       probability of the spinner
       (i) stopping on section C when it is spun once
       (ii) not stopping on section B when it is spun once.
   (c) Explain whether or not there is evidence to suggest
       that the spinner might be biased.

3 In a batch of 1000 mugs produced in a pottery, seven are
   found to be cracked.
   Work out an estimate of the probability of a mug not
   being cracked.

4 An airline checks the departure times of 200 flights. Of the
   200 flights
       12 are early, 142 are on time and the remainder are late.
   Use this evidence to work out the best estimate of the
   probability that a randomly selected flight departs late.

5 George throws a coin 100 times.
   It lands heads 57 times.
   Jane throws the same coin 100 times.
   It lands heads 45 times.
   (a) Explain why George and Jane's results are not the
       same.
   (b) Explain whether or not there is sufficient evidence to
       suggest that the coin is biased.

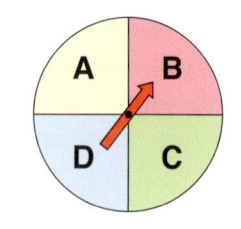

Mixed exercise 6

1 Tristan has ten marbles in a bag.
Six of the marbles are red, three are blue, and one is white.
He picks a marble at random.
Write down the probability that the marble he picks is
 (a) white
 (b) blue
 (c) either blue or white
 (d) yellow.

2 The diagram represents a fair spinner in the shape of a regular hexagon.
The sections of the spinner are labelled with letters.
The spinner is spun once.
Write down the probability that it lands on a section marked
 (a) A
 (b) B
 (c) C
 (d) D.

3 This spinner is spun once.
 (a) On which colour is it most likely to land?
     Give a reason for your answer.
 (b) Copy the probability scale.
     Mark with an X the probability that the spinner lands on red.

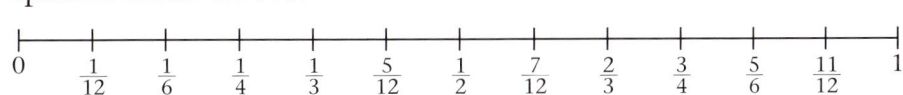

$0 \quad \frac{1}{12} \quad \frac{1}{6} \quad \frac{1}{4} \quad \frac{1}{3} \quad \frac{5}{12} \quad \frac{1}{2} \quad \frac{7}{12} \quad \frac{2}{3} \quad \frac{3}{4} \quad \frac{5}{6} \quad \frac{11}{12} \quad 1$

 (c) Write down the probability that it lands on white.

4 This four-sided dice is biased. Its vertices are labelled 1 to 4.
Here are Jim's estimates for the probability of getting each score.

Score	1	2	3	4
Estimated probability	0.28	0.31	0.26	0.23

Explain why these estimates cannot all be correct.

5 Ben's bus to work can be **late**, **on time** or **early**.
The probability of it being late is 0.26.
The probability of it being on time is 0.65.
Work out the probability of Ben's bus being early.

6 A bag contains 12 equal-sized coloured balls. Five of the balls are red, four are blue and three are white.
Work out the probability of the selected ball being
(a) blue
(b) either red or blue
(c) green
(d) not red.

7 The probability of Jenny winning the raffle is $\frac{3}{1000}$.
Work out the probability of Jenny not winning the raffle.

8 The probability of a new DVD being faulty is 0.002.
(a) Work out the probability of a new DVD not being faulty.
(b) A batch of 30 000 DVDs is released.
Estimate the number of faulty DVDs in this batch.

9 The probability of Lola getting an A* in Mathematics is 96%.
Work out the probability of Lola not getting an A* in Mathematics.

10 A biased dice is rolled once. The probabilities for some scores are:

Score	1	2	3	4	5	6
Probability	0.13	0.17	0.18	0.12		0.20

(a) Work out the probability of a score of 5.
(b) Work out the probability of a score less than 4.
(c) Work out the probability of a score that is a prime number.

11 Joshua rolls an ordinary dice once.
It has faces marked 1, 2, 3, 4, 5 and 6.
(a) Write down the probability that he gets
(i) a 6
(ii) an odd number
(iii) a number less than 3
(iv) an 8.

Ken rolls a different dice 60 times.
This dice also has six faces.
The table gives information about Ken's scores.

Score on dice	Frequency
1	9
2	11
3	20
4	2
5	8
6	10

(b) Explain what you think is different about Ken's dice. [E]

12 On the school sports day Patrick enters the 100 metres and the long jump.

It is estimated that
  the probability of Patrick winning the 100 metres = 0.7
  the probability of Patrick winning the long jump = 0.5.

Explain fully what is wrong with the following statement:
  'The probability of Patrick winning the 100 metres or the long jump = 0.7 + 0.5 = 1.2'

13 A football team can win, lose or draw a match.
The team plays two matches.
List all the possible joint outcomes of the two matches.

14 A game is played with these two fair spinners.
   (a) Draw a sample space diagram to show all the possible joint outcomes when the spinners are each spun once.
   (b) Work out the probability of the joint outcome (red, 3).

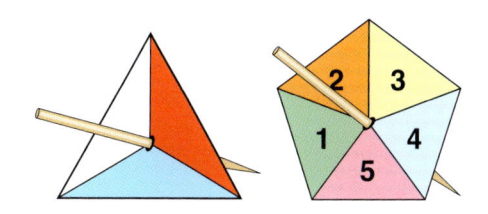

15 A sandwich bar offers all fillings in one of three options:
  wrap   baguette   sliced bread.
The five fillings are:
  chicken, tuna, cheese, ham, hummus.
One possible sandwich is hummus in a wrap.
Draw a sample space diagram to show all the possible sandwich options.

16 Jim spins the spinner shown in the diagram twice.
He records the sum of the two scores.
   (a) Copy and complete this table to show all the possible results.

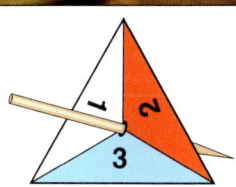

          2nd spin
	1	2	3
1			
2			5
3			

1st spin

   (b) Work out the probability of a score of
      (i) 6   (ii) 3   (iii) 8.

17 A market research team conducts a survey into the main method of travel people used to travel to their holiday destination.
They choose a random sample of 1200 people taken from across the country. The results of the survey are shown in the table below.

Method of travel	Plane	Coach	Train	Car	Did not go on holiday
Frequency	451	106	124	474	45

(a) Work out the best estimate for the probability that someone, chosen at random
  (i) did not go on holiday
  (ii) did **not** travel to their holiday destination by train.

There are approximately 700 000 people in Maidford.

(b) Work out the estimate of the most likely number of people who went on holiday by car.

18 The diagram shows a biased spinner.
Michael spins the spinner 100 times.
His results are:

Letter	A	B	C	D	E
Frequency	17	26	31	9	17

Jenny spins the spinner 200 times.
Her results are:

Letter	A	B	C	D	E
Frequency	39	48	69	21	23

(a) Jenny spins the spinner twice as many times as Michael.
Explain why the frequencies in Jenny's table are not twice those in Michael's table.

(b) Work out the best estimate of the probability of the spinner stopping on the sections marked
  (i) B   (ii) D   (iii) with a vowel
when it is spun once.

(c) The spinner is spun 1000 times.
Work out an estimate for the likely number of times it will land on D.

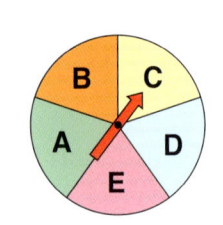

> Use your estimate for P(D) from part **(b)**.

19 The diagram represents a spinner.
The spinner was spun 10 000 times and the faces it stopped on were recorded. The results were:

Face	A	B	C	D	E
No. of times	593	4009	1427	2003	1968

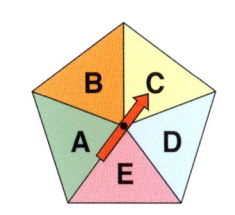

Explain clearly whether or not this information suggests that the spinner is biased.

Summary of key points

1 An event that is *certain* to happen has a **probability of 1**.

2 An event that *cannot happen* has a **probability of 0**.

3 The probability that an event will happen is always greater than or equal to 0 (impossible) and less than or equal to 1 (certain).
This can be written:
$$0 \leqslant \text{probability} \leqslant 1$$

4 If all the possible outcomes of an event are equally likely, the probability that the event will happen is
$$\text{probability} = \frac{\text{number of successful outcomes}}{\text{total number of possible outcomes}}$$

5 Outcomes are **mutually exclusive** when they cannot happen at the same time.

6 A **sample space diagram** shows all possible outcomes of one or more events.

7 The probabilities of all the mutually exclusive outcomes of an event add to 1.

8 The probability of an event **not** happening = 1 − probability of the event happening.
$$P(\text{not } A) = 1 - P(A)$$

9 The **relative frequency** of an outcome in an experiment is
$$\text{relative frequency} = \frac{\text{number of successful trials}}{\text{total number of trials}}$$

10 For a trial or experiment, the **estimated probability** is given by the relative frequency.

Examination practice paper

Section A (calculator)

1. Ann bought a bag of sweets.

   She counted the number of red, yellow, orange and green sweets.

   Here are her results.

Colour	Number of sweets
Red	7
Yellow	4
Orange	8
Green	2

   On a copy of the grid, draw a bar chart to show to this information.

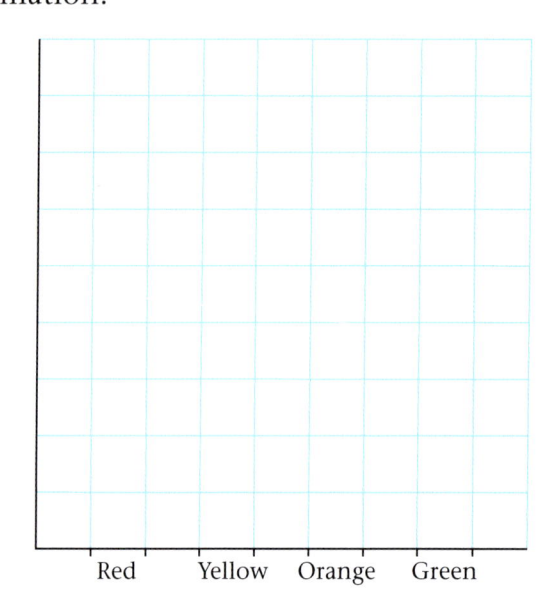

   (2 marks)

2. Haleem made a list of his homework marks.

   9   8   3   5   7   8   6   8   8   8

   (a) Write down the range of his homework marks.

   (1 mark)

   (b) Write down the mode of his homework marks.

   (1 mark)

   (c) Work out his mean homework mark.   (3 marks)

3 The table gives information about the types of central heating used by households in a village.

Type of central heating	Frequency	
Electricity	6	
Gas	42	
Oil	24	

Copy and complete this diagram.
Draw an accurate pie chart to show this information.

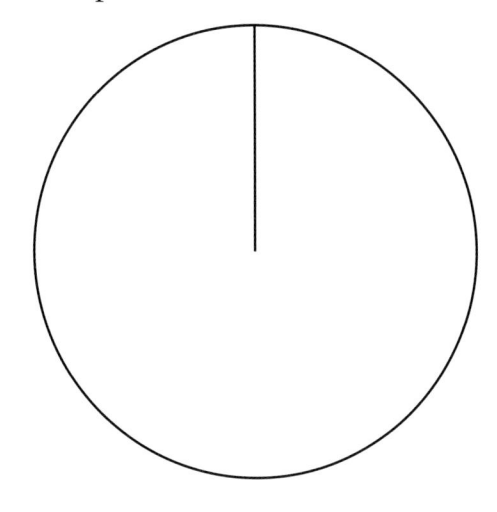

(4 marks)

4 A bag contains yellow, red and blue balls.

Carl takes one ball at random from the bag.

The table shows the probabilities that Carl takes a yellow ball or a red ball.

Colour	Yellow	Red	Blue
Probability	0.25	0.3	

(a) Work out the probability that Carl takes a yellow ball or a red ball. **(2 marks)**

(b) Work out the probability that Carl takes a blue ball.
(2 marks)

Total for Section A: 15 marks

Section B (non-calculator)

1 Josh carried out a survey of his friends' favourite flavour of crisps.

   Here are his results.

Salt and vinegar	Cheese and onion	Plain
Bacon	Plain	Bacon
Plain	Cheese and onion	Salt and vinegar
Cheese and onion	Cheese and onion	Salt and vinegar
Salt and vinegar	Bacon	Cheese and onion
Cheese and onion	Plain	Salt and vinegar
Cheese and onion	Cheese and onion	Plain
Bacon	Bacon	Plain
Bacon		

   (a) Copy and complete the table to show Josh's results.

Flavour of crisps	Tally	Frequency
Salt and vinegar		
Cheese and onion		
Plain		
Bacon		

   (2 marks)

   (b) Write down the number of Josh's friends whose favourite flavour was bacon. **(1 mark)**

   (c) Which flavour is the most popular among Josh's friends? **(1 mark)**

2 The diagram shows a fair spinner in the shape of a regular hexagon.

   The spinner can land on A or B or C.

   Lindsey spins the spinner.

   (a) On which letter is the spinner most likely to land? Explain your answer. **(2 marks)**

   (b) Write down the probability that the spinner will land on A. **(1 mark)**

3 Fiona says

   'The median of a set of data is the value which occurs most often.'

   She is **wrong**. Explain why. **(1 mark)**

4 150 people each win a prize.

They win one of a badge, a flag or sticker.

The two-way table shows some information about the prizes they win.

Copy and complete the two-way table.

	Badge	Flag	Sticker	Total
Male	27			81
Female	15		17	
Total		68		150

(3 marks)

5 The scatter graph shows information about the height and arm span for nine students.

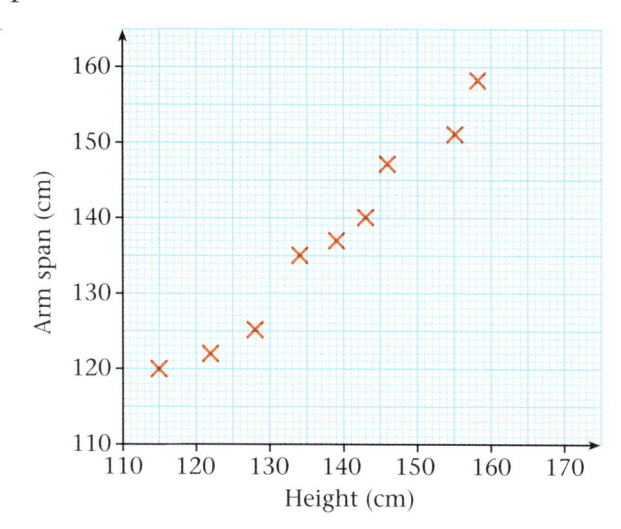

Another student has a height of 130 cm and an arm span of 134 cm.

(a) Plot this information on a copy of the scatter graph. **(1 mark)**

(b) What type of correlation does this scatter graph show? **(1 mark)**

(c) Draw a line of best fit on your copy of the scatter graph. **(1 mark)**

The height of another student is 150 cm.

(d) Use your line of best fit to find an estimate for the arm span of this student. **(1 mark)**

Total for Section B: 15 marks

Answers

Exercise 1A

1. A
2. B
3. C
4. A
5. (a) Everyone in the school.
   (b) The results are accurate.
   (c) There is a lot of data to process.
6. (a) (c) and (f) secondary; (b), (d) and (e) primary

Exercise 1B

1. List the types of sweet available. Give numberical options regarding how many of each type are consumed per week on average.
2. (a) D He can then calculate how far people have travelled (people might not know the actual distances they've travelled). This way will also show if there is one particular area for which the cafe is very popular.
   (b) More people than on average for other days might use the internet cafe on a Friday and therefore his results might be a little exaggerated.
3. (a) The questions omits many possible methods of communication and cannot be answered by the Yes/No tick boxes.
   (b) The number of e-mail addresses is not relevant to how teenagers communicate with each other.
4. The question should specify a time period, e.g. each week. The options are too specific. They should give a range, for example: less than £1, £1 to £1.99, £2 to £2.99, £3 to £3.99, £4 or more.

Exercise 1C

1. (a) Continuous   (b) Discrete
   (c) Discrete   (d) Continuous
   (e) Continuous

2.
Number of bids	Tally	Frequency
1–5	⊮ I	6
6–10	⊮ ⊮ I	11
11–15	IIII	4
16–20	III	3

3.
Height, h (m)	Tally	Frequency
$0 \leq w < 5$	IIII	4
$5 \leq w < 10$	⊮ IIII	9
$10 \leq w < 15$	⊮ ⊮ I	11
$15 \leq w < 20$	IIII	4
$20 \leq w < 25$	II	2

4.
Drink	Tally	Frequency
Beer	⊮ ⊮ II	12
Wine	⊮ III	3
Spirits	⊮ I	6
Sherry	⊮ IIII	9

5.
Temperature	Tally	Frequency
$15 \leq t < 16$	II	2
$16 \leq t < 17$	III	3
$17 \leq t < 18$	⊮ I	6
$18 \leq t < 19$	⊮ ⊮ I	11
$19 \leq t < 20$	⊮	5
$20 \leq t < 21$	⊮	5
$21 \leq t < 22$	IIII	4
$22 \leq t < 23$	IIII	4

6.
Type of car	Tally	Frequency
Vauxhall		
Rover		
BMW		
...		
...		
(etc.)		

7.
Type of music	Tally	Frequency
Classical		
Pop		
Jazz		
Rock		
...		
...		
(etc.)		

Exercise 1D

1.
	School lunch	Packed lunch	Other	Total
Female	21	13	13	47
Male	19	5	14	38
Total	40	18	27	85

2.
	Walks	Cycle	Car	Bus	Total
KS3					
KS4					
Sixth form					
Total					

3.
	Jazz	Rock	Classical	Folk	Total
Men	12	17	19	4	52
Women	9	23	9	7	48
Total	21	40	28	11	100

Answers 93

4

Age (years)	Male	Female	Total
21–30	1	2	3
31–40	4	6	10
41–50	11	1	12
51–60	7	3	10
Total	23	12	35

Mixed exercise 1

1 (a) Mileage is continuous so we should group the data. We will use a class interval of 5000 miles. We know there are no cars with mileage less than 10000 or greater than 100000, so our sheet will only be between these mileages. We use tallies and frequencies.

(b)

Mileage in thousands (m)	Tally	Frequency
$10 \leq m < 15$	|||	3
$15 \leq m < 20$	|||||		6
$20 \leq m < 25$	||||	4
$25 \leq m < 30$	||	2
$30 \leq m < 35$	|||	3
$35 \leq m < 40$			1
$40 \leq m < 45$	||||	4
$45 \leq m < 50$	||	2
$50 \leq m < 55$	||	2
$55 \leq m < 60$	|||	3
$60 \leq m < 65$	||	2
$65 \leq m < 70$			1
$70 \leq m < 75$		0
$75 \leq m < 80$	||	2
$80 \leq m < 85$			1
$85 \leq m < 90$	||	2
$90 \leq m < 95$			1
$95 \leq m < 100$			1

2 (a) We will record the min. and max. temperatures in separate tables. Since the data is continuous we will group the data. We will use a class interval of 5°C. The max. temperature is not lower than 15°C or higher than 45°C, and the min. temperature is not lower than 10°C or higher than 30°C, so these are the ranges we will use. We use tallies and frequencies.

(b)

Max. temperature (T) in °C	Tally	Frequency
$15 \leq T < 20$	|||	3
$20 \leq T < 25$	|||	3
$25 \leq T < 30$	||||	4
$30 \leq T < 35$	|||	3
$35 \leq T < 40$			1
$40 \leq T < 45$			1

Min. temperature (T) in °C	Tally	Frequency
$10 \leq t < 15$	|||||	5
$15 \leq t < 20$	||	2
$20 \leq t < 25$	|||||	5
$25 \leq t < 30$	|||	3

3 She should have two separate tables for boys and girls. She will need to group the data, since times are continuous. A class interval of 1 hour would be OK. She will need to allow for times from 0 to 28 hours or more.

4 He needs to specify a time period, e.g. each week or each month. People will not all mean the same by 'a few' and 'a lot' so he needs to give numbers, e.g. 0–2, 3–5, …

5

	French	German	Spanish	Total
Female	15	11	13	39
Male	16	17	8	41
Total	31	28	21	80

Exercise 2A

1 (a)

Car	Tally	Frequency
Ford	||||| ||||| |||||		16
Skoda			1
Vauxhall	|||||		6
Jaguar	|||	3
BMW	|||	3
Fiat	|||	3
Rover	|||||	5
Honda	|||	3

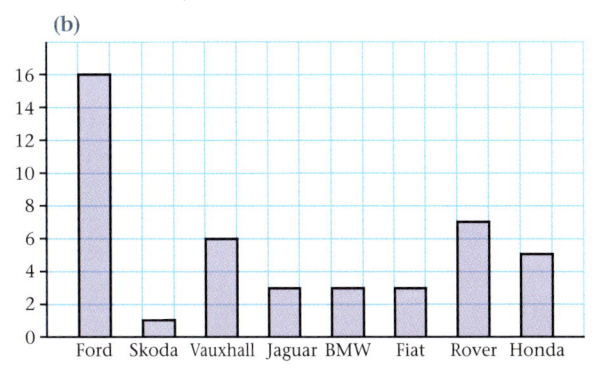

(b) [Bar chart showing frequencies: Ford 16, Skoda 1, Vauxhall 6, Jaguar 3, BMW 3, Fiat 3, Rover 7, Honda 5]

(c) Ford

2 (a) 30   **(b)** 40

(c) Wed

Answers

3 (a) Wednesday (b) 6
(c)

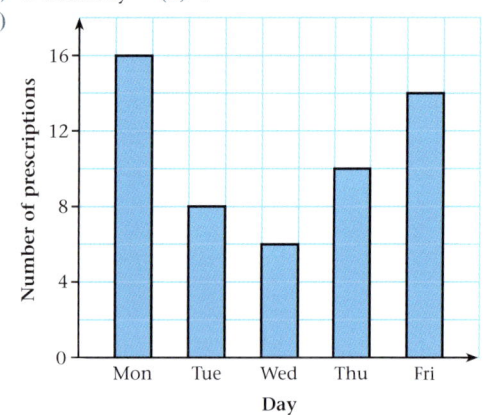

(d) 54

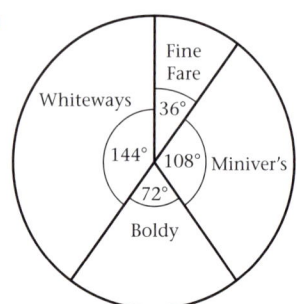

(b)

Subject	Frequency	Angle
Whiteways	36	144°
Baldy	18	72°
Miniver's	27	108°
Fine Fare	9	36°
Total	90	360°

(c) (i) Whiteways (ii) Fine Fare

4

5

Exercise 2B

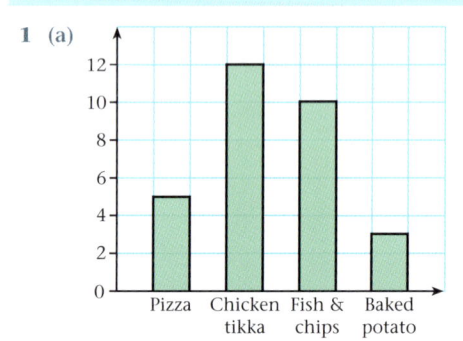

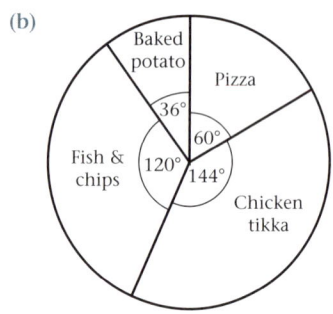

1 (a)

(b)

2 (a) Badminton
(b) 15 people
(c) $\frac{1}{12}$

3 (a)

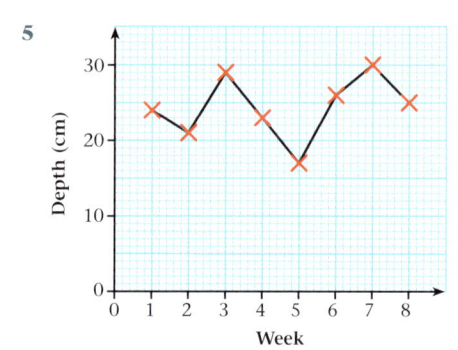

Exercise 2C

1
```
3 | 2, 8
4 | 2, 3, 4, 8, 9
5 | 0, 1, 1, 2, 4, 4, 5, 5, 7, 7, 7
6 | 1, 1, 2, 2, 2, 3, 3, 3, 4, 4, 6, 7, 9
7 | 0, 1, 2, 2, 7
8 | 0, 5
9 | 0, 1           Key: 3|2 means 32
```

2 (a)
```
0 | 6, 8
1 | 2, 5, 6, 7, 9
2 | 0, 2, 5, 6, 7, 7, 9, 9
3 | 1, 2, 2, 3, 3, 4, 6, 8, 8, 8, 9
4 | 0, 1, 2, 2, 4, 5, 6, 6, 6, 6, 8, 8, 9, 9
5 | 0, 1, 2, 2, 2, 3, 4, 4, 6, 6, 7, 9
6 | 1, 1, 1, 4, 4
7 | 0, 3
8 | 2              Key: 3|1 means 31
```
(b) No, there are more in their 40s than any other age group.

3
```
14 | 9
15 | 9
16 | 4, 7, 8, 8, 9, 9
17 | 0, 1, 2, 3, 3, 3, 6, 7, 9, 9
18 | 1, 2, 3, 3, 4, 5, 6, 6, 8
19 | 1, 2
20 | 1            Key: 14|9 means 149
```

Answers

Exercise 2D

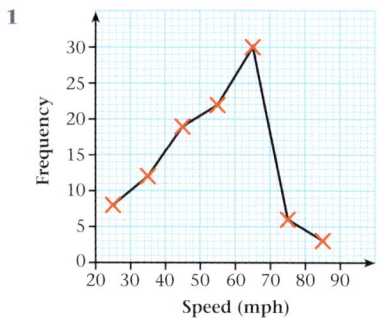

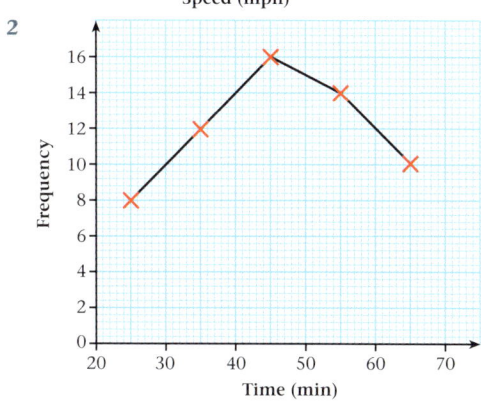

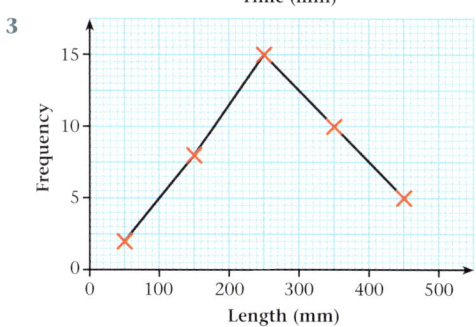

1 Frequency polygon with points at (25,8), (35,12), (45,19), (55,22), (65,30), (75,6), (85,3) against Speed (mph).

2 Frequency polygon with points at (25,8), (35,12), (45,16), (55,14), (65,10) against Time (min).

3 Frequency polygon with points at (50,2), (150,8), (250,15), (350,10), (450,5) against Length (mm).

Mixed exercise 2

1 (a)

Type of music	Tally	Frequency
Pop	|||| |||| |||| |||	18
Classical	|||	3
Jazz	|||| ||	7
Rock	|||| |||| ||	12

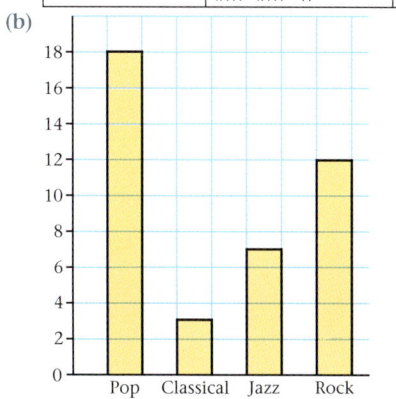

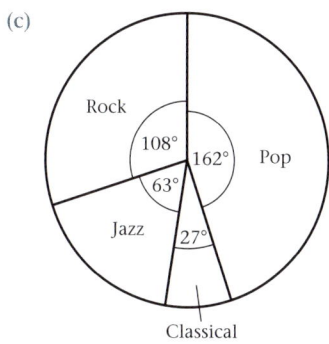

(b) Bar chart: Pop 18, Classical 3, Jazz 7, Rock 12.

(c) Pie chart: Rock 108°, Pop 162°, Jazz 63°, Classical 27°.

2 (a) 12 **(b)** 3

(c)
Jan	⊕ ⊕ ⊕
Feb	⊕ ⌓
Mar	⊕ ⊕
Apr	⊕ ⊕ ⊕ ⊕ ⊕
May	⊕ ⊕ ⊕ ⌓

3 (a)

	UK	Europe	Elsewhere	Total
July	**12**	20	8	40
Aug	36	**48**	16	**100**
Sept	**8**	32	**20**	60
Total	56	100	44	**200**

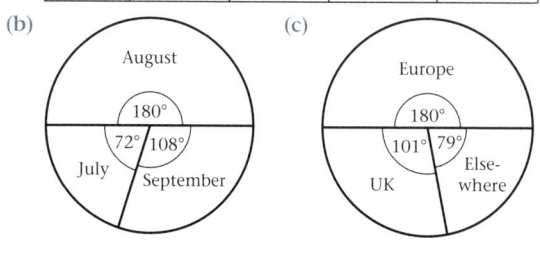

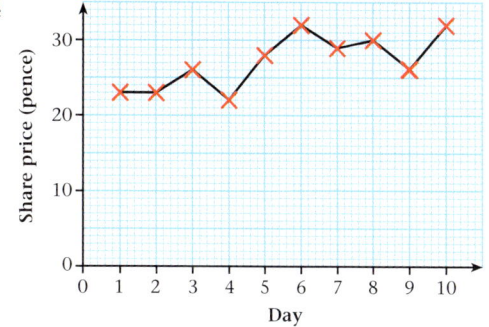

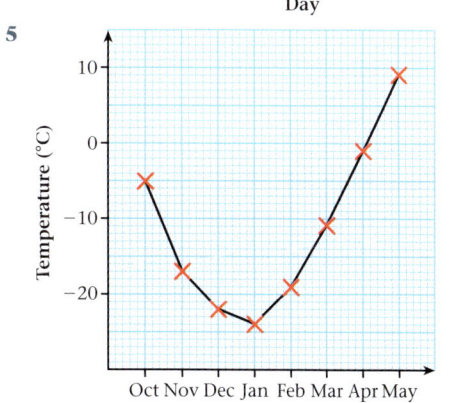

(b) Pie chart: August 180°, July 72°, September 108°.

(c) Pie chart: Europe 180°, UK 101°, Elsewhere 79°.

4 Line graph of Share price (pence) vs Day: (1,23), (2,23), (3,26), (4,22), (5,28), (6,32), (7,29), (8,30), (9,26), (10,32).

5 Line graph of Temperature (°C) vs month: Oct −5, Nov −17, Dec −23, Jan −24, Feb −19, Mar −11, Apr −1, May 9.

96 Answers

6

Colour	Frequency
Silver	18
Black	12
Red	30
Blue	20
White	40

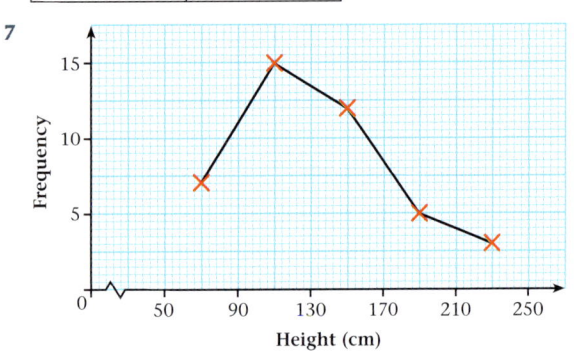

7 Frequency polygon with points plotted at approximately (70, 7), (110, 15), (150, 12), (190, 5), (230, 3); x-axis: Height (cm) from 50 to 250; y-axis: Frequency 0 to 15.

8

Weight, w (kg)	Frequency
$40 < w \leq 50$	4
$50 < w \leq 60$	6
$60 < w \leq 70$	4
$70 < w \leq 80$	7
$80 < w \leq 90$	6

9
```
 9 | 9
10 | 9
11 | 0, 0, 0, 1, 5, 8
12 | 0, 0, 5, 5, 5, 7, 7
13 | 2, 4
14 | 1, 9
15 | 9
16 | 3, 9
17 | 0
18 | 0
```
Key: 10|9 means 109

Exercise 3A
1 (a) 1 (b) 6 (c) 11.16 (d) 58
2 (a) 8 (b) 7.25 (c) 6.71 (d) 5
3 (a) 171 min (b) 69 min (c) 168.8 min
4 (a) 25 (b) 36 (c) 28
5 6.5
6 40 kg to 50 kg

Exercise 3B
1 (a) 2 goals (b) 1 goal (c) 1.35 goals
2 (a) 4 days (b) 0.81 days
3 (a) 1 (b) 1.36
4 (a) 4 people (b) 4.01 people (c) 6 people

Exercise 3C
1 (a) 3 to 5 messages (b) 3 to 5 messages
  (c) 4.68 messages
2 (a) 237.5 g (b) $200 < w \leq 300$ g
  (c) $100 < w \leq 200$ g (d) 500 g

3 (a) Estimate mean speed is 38.4 mph (3 s.f.)
  (b) $40 < s \leq 50$ mph (c) $30 < s \leq 40$ mph
  (d) 21 vehicles

Activity – Estimating the mean
1 Frequencies: 5, 8, 9, 13, 1, 9, 5
2 Estimated mean: 63.8 seconds
3 Frequencies: 8, 14, 13, 10, 5
  Estimated mean: 64.5 seconds
5 Mean: 63.1 seconds
6 Estimating the mean makes the assumption that the values are uniformly distributed within the class intervals. As values are not uniformly distributed, the estimated mean will depend on the class intervals chosen.

Mixed exercise 3
1 (a) 13 (b) 13
2 (a) 2 (b) 28 cm²
3 (a)

Length in cm	Tally	Frequency
2	|	1
3	|	1
4	||||	4
5	卌 |	6
6	|||	3
7	|||	3
8	||	2

  (b) 5 cm (c) 6 cm

4 (a)

Temperature, T (°C)	Tally	Frequency
$15 \leq T < 20$	||	2
$20 \leq T < 25$	卌 |	6
$25 \leq T < 30$	卌 卌 ||	12
$30 \leq T < 35$	||||	4
$35 \leq T < 40$	|	1

  (b) Median temperature = 26°C
  (c) Modal class interval is $25 \leq T < 30$
  (d) Mean temperature = 26.28°C
5 (a) Fifth number = 11 (b) Median = 9
6 (a) 30 (b) 3 (c) 30.2
7 (a) Mean speed = 63.2 mph (1 d.p.)
  (b) Mean speed = 63.5 mph
  (c) Range = 51 mph
  (d)

Speed, s (mph)	Tally	Frequency
$30 \leq s < 40$	|	1
$40 \leq s < 50$	|||	3
$50 \leq s < 60$	卌 ||	7
$60 \leq s < 70$	卌 ||||	9
$70 \leq s < 80$	卌 ||	7
$80 \leq s < 90$	|||	3

  (e) Modal class interval is $60 \leq s < 70$ mph
8 Overall mean = 8.6 years
9 (a) 50 to 55 years (b) 45 to 50 years
10 The highest mark was 18 so the lowest mark was 10. The mean lies between the highest and lowest marks.
11 The greatest possible time of any track is 500 seconds so the mean must be less than 500 seconds.
12 (a) $35 \leq t < 40$ (b) 34.75 min or 34 min 45 sec

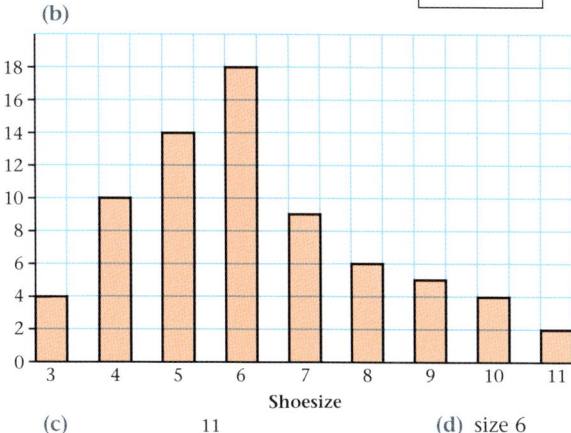

Exercise 4A

1. (a) £599
   (b) Costa Brava, Paris, Barcelona, Edinburgh
   (c) Austria, Costa Brava
   (d) Majorca
2. (a) Sumreen (b) Fiona (c) Gary, Asif
3. (a) (i) 3110 miles (ii) 4259 miles
   (b) Athens and Cairo
   (c) Athens and Hong Kong
   (d) 6539 miles

Exercise 4B

1. During the first 3 years the value of the 2000 cc car was greater than that of the 1200 cc car.
   At 3 years old the value of the cars was the same.
   The greatest difference in value was at the start.
   During the final 5 years the 1200 cc car was the more valuable.
2. The difference in average house prices between the two regions was least in year 5 and greatest in year 10.
   Average house prices were consistently higher in region A.
   Average house prices in both regions had increased at the end of the 10-year period.
3. (a) 2 hours (b) Wednesday
   (c) (i) 9 hours (ii) Helen (11 hours)
4. (a) August (b) 1.5 °C
   (c) Throughout the period April to October temperatures in Barcelona were higher than in London.

Exercise 4C

1. The median mark for the boys was higher than for the girls. However, the spread was greater for the girls than for the boys, so some girls may have received higher marks than any of the boys.
2. To reach any conclusion we need to know which measure of average was used, and we need a measure of spread. For example consider the girls' marks of 1, 2, 4, 5 and 5 with the boys' marks of 3, 3, 3, 6 and 8.
   The mode and median for the girls are higher than for the boys, but the boys' marks are better than the girls'.
   Or consider girls' marks of 8, 9 and 10, with mean of 9, and boys' marks of 0, 12, and 12 with mean of 8.
   The girls' mean is higher, but two of the three boys had higher marks than all three girls, so it is not possible to conclude that the girls rated the product higher than the boys.
3. Nick was the better player. They each won 2 matches but Nick had the lower average score and a smaller range than Tiger, so he is a more consistent player.

Mixed exercise 4

1. (a) 4539 km (b) Chicago (c) Boston
3. You cannot know whether the people at Creswell Ltd are better paid. There may be one highly paid manager whose salary raises the mean wage, while most of the staff have lower wages than at Spencer and Sons.
4. (a) 150
   (b) If the ice cream seller was outside, bad weather may have kept people indoors. If the ice cream seller was at an indoor venue, beautiful weather may have persuaded people to stay outside.
5. The modal price range for Make A cars is £15 000–£20 000, compared to £5000–£10 000 for Make B.
   There were more Make B than Make A in the under £5000 and £5000–£10 000 price ranges and more Make A than Make B cars in all the higher price ranges.
6. For example
   The mode grade in 2004 was C.
   The mode grade in 2005 was B.
   The percentage of students getting grades A*–B has gone up from 36% in 2004 to 39% in 2005.
7. For example
   Ali generally has more cars at a particular range than Nick; an exception to this is for cars of value £0–£2000.
   The price range where the difference in the number of cars they have is greatest, is £8000–£9000.
   The price range where the difference in the number of cars they have is smallest, is £7000–£8000.
8. (a)

Shoe size	Tally	Frequency
3	IIII	4
4	HHT HHT	10
5	HHT HHT IIII	14
6	HHT HHT HHT III	18
7	HHT IIII	9
8	HHT I	6
9	HHT	5
10	IIII	4
11	II	2
Total		72

   (b) [bar chart of shoe size frequencies]
   (c) [pie chart with angles 10°, 20°, 20°, 25°, 30°, 45°, 50°, 70°]
   (d) size 6
   (e) There is not sufficient evidence, as there might be more students with shoe size between 3 and 6 at the other school than at Dominique's school. Also sample size must be known, as well as range, etc.
9. (a) 1 348 000 000, is much larger than the other populations.
   (b) The median would truly reflect the average population. The mean will not since the exceptional value will affect it. It does not make sence to use the mode since the data is not grouped.

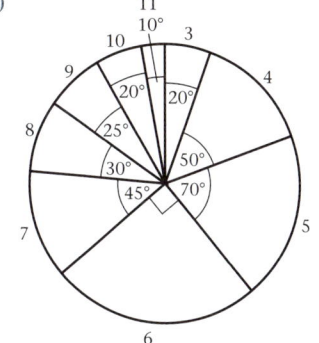

Answers

(c)
```
 0  | 2, 3, 4, 4, 4, 5, 5, 9
 1  | 0, 0, 0, 0, 3, 6
 2  | 2
 3  | 8, 9
 4  | 1, 5, 9
 5  | 8, 9
 6  | 0
 7  | 0
 8  | 2
 9  |
10  | 0
11  |
12  | 7
13  |
14  | 2, 7
15  |
16  |
17  | 6
⋮
28  | 7
⋮
134 | 8      Key: 8|2 means 82
```

(d) Out of the seven countries Uruguay has the largest number of wins per million people; we expect that the higher this is, the better the country is at football. Despite having a small population, Uruguay have found footballers good enough to win the World Cup two times.

Exercise 5A

1 (a) and (c)

(b) Correlation between mileage and value is negative.
(d) (i) 50 000 miles (ii) £3100

2 (a) and (c)

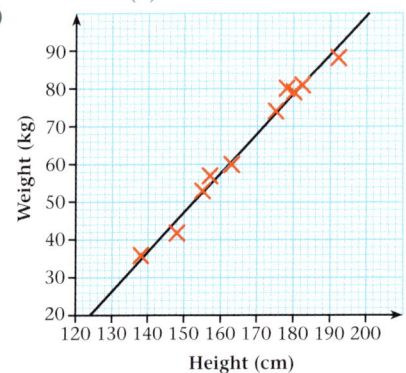

(b) Positive correlation between height and weight of these people.
(d) (i) 47 kg (ii) 174 cm

Exercise 5B

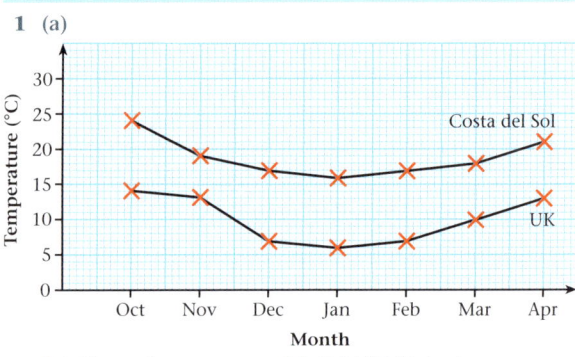

1 (a)

(b) November (c) 8.86 °C (2 d.p.)

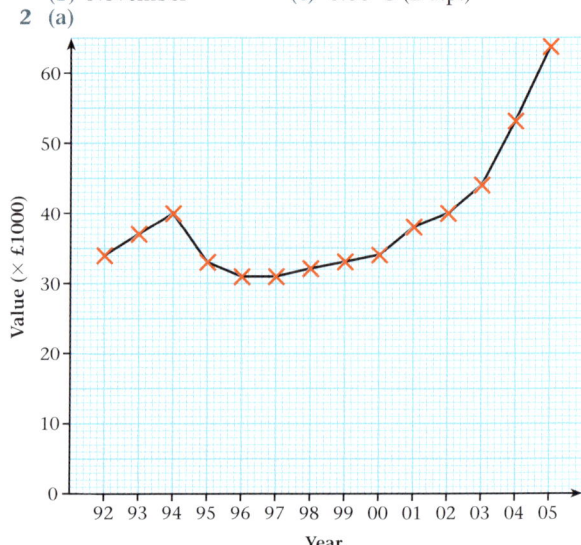

2 (a)

(b) Between 1992 and 1994 the value increased steadily.
Between 1994 and 1995 the value sharply decreased, to lower than the value when Wendy bought the house.
The value of the house was lowest in 1996 and 1997, but between 1997 and 2000 the value slowly increased.
Between 2000 and 2005 the value increased very sharply, and from 2001 it increased by more each year, to its highest point in 2005.

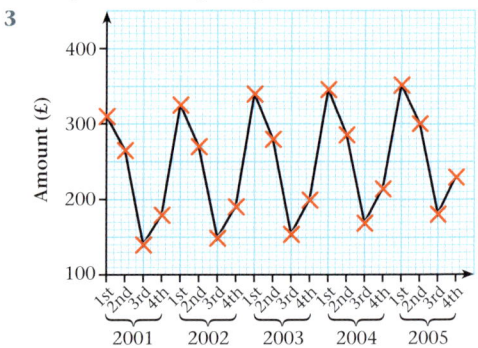

3

Answers

4

[Graph: Amount (£ 1000) vs months J A J O across 2001–2005, showing oscillating pattern between ~110 and ~270]

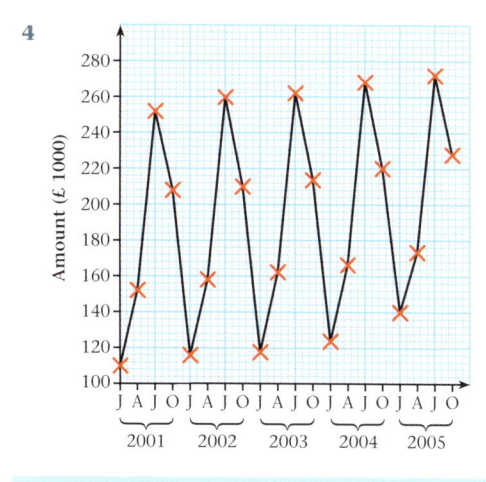

Exercise 5C

1 £15 725.02 **2** 76p

3 Assuming bread prices follow the changes in the RPI, a similar loaf would cost 4p.

4 (a) (b)

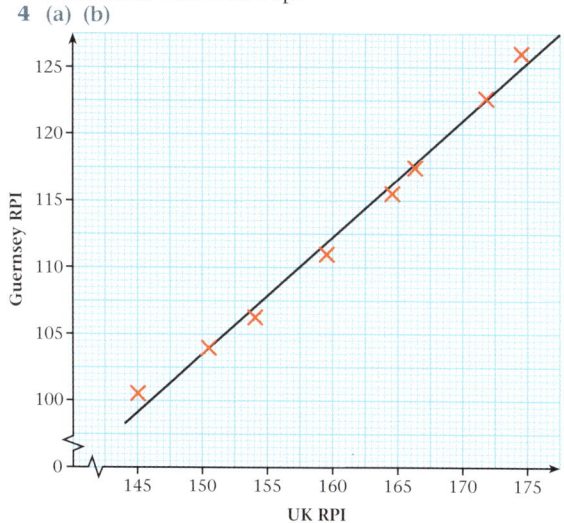

[Scatter graph: Guernsey RPI vs UK RPI, positive linear trend from (145, ~100) to (175, ~127)]

(c) Scatter graph shows positive correlation between the UK and Guernsey RPIs.

(d) Proportional changes to RPI have been:
For UK: $\frac{174.6}{145.0} = 1.204$ For Guernsey: $\frac{125.9}{100.2} = 1.256$

Change in RPI is less for UK than for Guernsey. So, no evidence to support claim.

Mixed exercise 5

1 (a), (c)

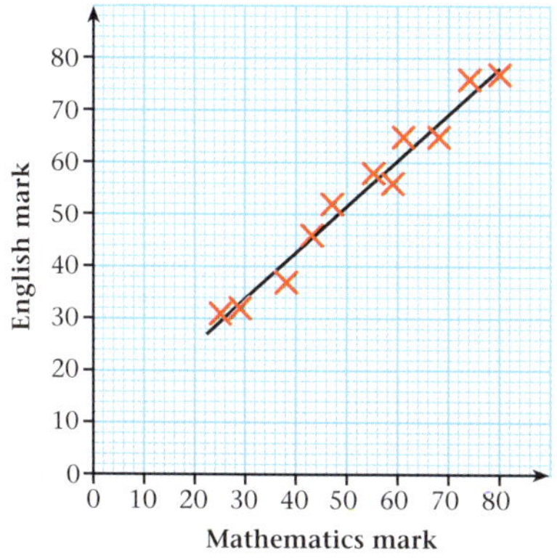

[Scatter graph: English mark vs Mathematics mark, positive correlation]

(b) There is a positive correlation between the marks scored in Mathematics and in English.

(d) 52 marks in English exam.

(e) Using 10s as the stem in both case, we have

(i) Mathematics

2	5, 9
3	8
4	3, 7
5	5, 9
6	1, 8
7	4
8	0

(ii) English

3	1, 2, 7
4	6
5	2, 6, 8
6	5, 5,
7	6, 7

Key: 2|5 means 25

2 (a), (c)

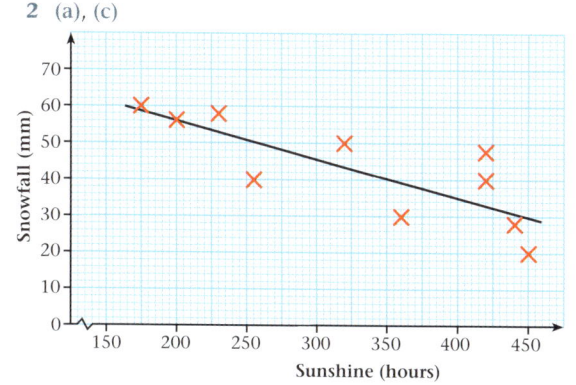

[Scatter graph: Snowfall (mm) vs Sunshine (hours), negative correlation]

(b) There is a negative correlation between the hours of sunshine and the snowfall.

(d)
2	0, 8
3	0
4	0, 0, 8
5	0, 6, 8
6	0

Key: 2|0 means 20

3 A – Negative, B – None, C – Positive

4 (a) The scatter diagram shows positive correlation

(b) [Scatter graph: Maths mark vs Science mark, positive correlation]

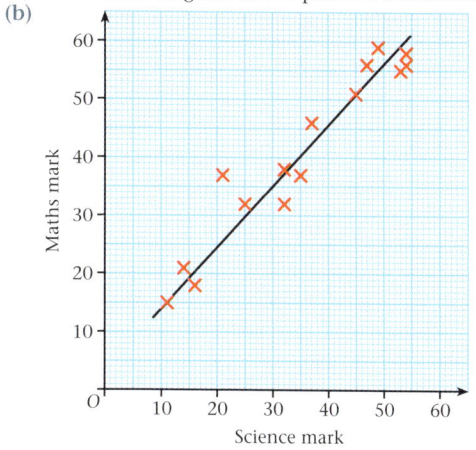

(b) 48 marks

5 The scatter diagram shows there is a positive correlation between value and area of floor space. There is one point on the scatter diagram which does not fit the correlation and is an exception (possibly due to the house being in a more expensive area than the others).

Answers

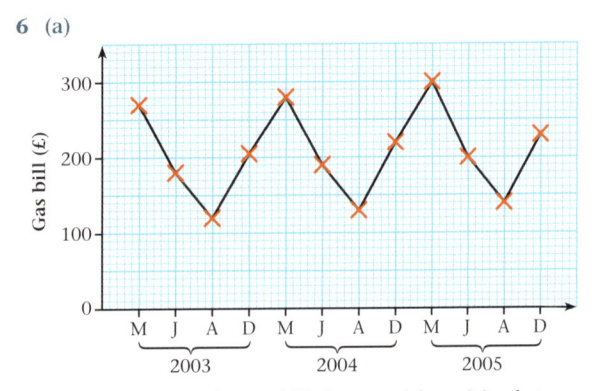

6 (a)

[Graph: Gas bill (£) vs months M J A D across 2003, 2004, 2005]

(b) In each year the gas bill decreased from March to August.
In each year the gas bill increased from August to March of the next year.
Comparing the same months in different years we see that the overall trend is an increase in the gas bill over the three years.

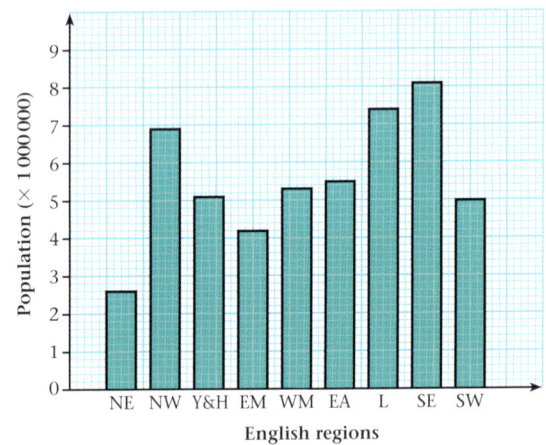

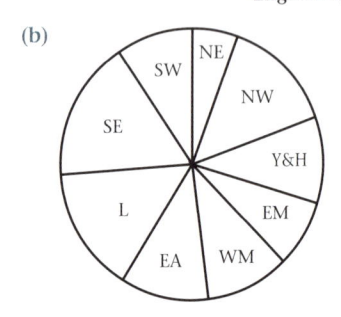

7 (a)

[Bar chart: Population (× 1 000 000) vs English regions: NE, NW, Y&H, EM, WM, EA, L, SE, SW]

(b) [Pie chart with sectors: NE, NW, Y&H, EM, WM, EA, L, SE, SW]

(c) South East

(d) £52 500, £61 000, £65 000, £68 850, £76 200, £82 500, £88 800, £120 000, £147 500

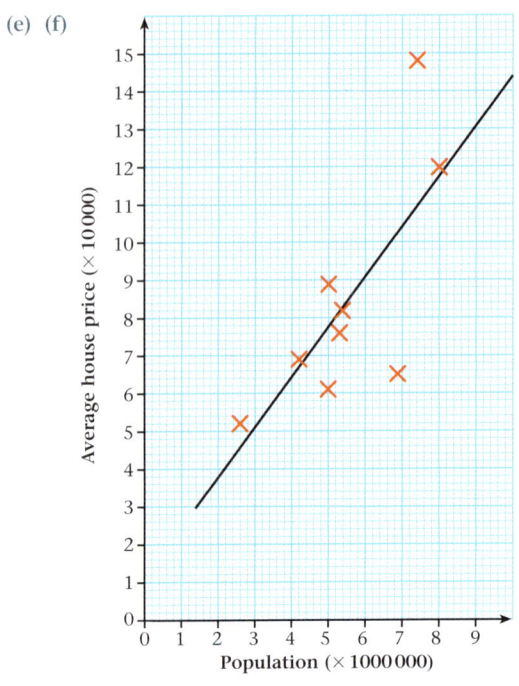

(e) (f) [Scatter graph: Average house price (× 10 000) vs Population (× 1 000 000) with line of best fit]

(g) There is a positive correlation between house prices and population.

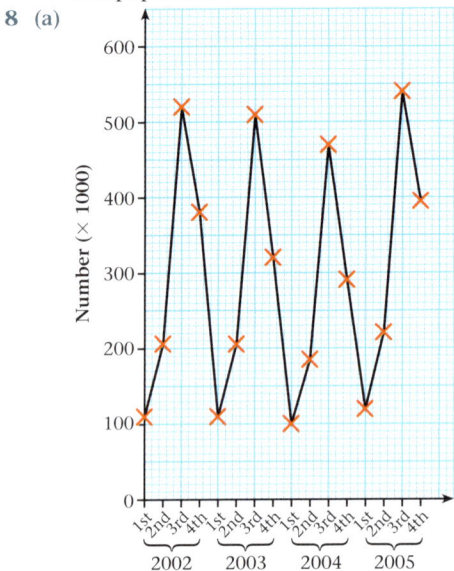

8 (a)

[Line graph: Number (× 1000) vs quarters 1st, 2nd, 3rd, 4th across 2002, 2003, 2004, 2005]

(b) In each year the bill is lowest in the first quarter. It increases in the second quarter, increases greatly in the third quarter then falls to the fourth quarter, and falls greatly to the first quarter of the next year.

Exercise 6A

1 [Probability scale: D at impossible, J at unlikely, T at evens, SC at certain]

2 [Number line 0 to 1: S at 0, T at ½, N at 1]

3 (a) B **(b)** A **(c)** C

4
```
S           H           M
|-----------|-----------|
0           1/2         1
```

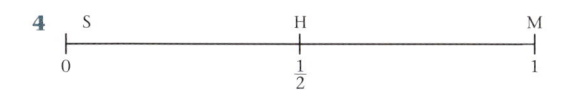

Exercise 6B

1 (a) $\frac{1}{3}$ (b) 0
2 (a) $\frac{1}{6}$ (b) $\frac{3}{6} = \frac{1}{2}$ (c) $\frac{3}{6} = \frac{1}{2}$ (d) 0
3 (a) $\frac{1}{15}$ (b) 0 (c) $\frac{6}{15}$ (d) $\frac{8}{15} + \frac{1}{15} = \frac{9}{15} = \frac{3}{5}$
4 (a) $\frac{1}{6}$ (b) $\frac{2}{6} = \frac{1}{3}$ (c) $\frac{3}{6} = \frac{1}{2}$ (d) 0

Exercise 6C

1 London by car   Manchester by car
   London by bus   Manchester by bus
   London by train   Manchester by train

   Bristol by car   Edinburgh by car
   Bristol by bus   Edinburgh by bus
   Bristol by train   Edinburgh by train

2 (a) (A, 1); (A, 2); (A, 3); (A, 4); (A, 5); (A, 6)
       (B, 1); (B, 2); (B, 3); (B, 4); (B, 5); (B, 6)
       (C, 1); (C, 2); (C, 3); (C, 4); (C, 5); (C, 6)
   (b) $\frac{1}{18}$ (c) $\frac{1}{18}$
3 (a) (R, 1); (R, 2); (R, 3)
       (B, 1); (B, 2); (B, 3)
       (W, 1); (W, 2); (W, 3)
   (b) $\frac{1}{9}$
4 (a) (H, 1) (H, 2) (H, 3) (H, 4) (H, 5) (H, 6)
       (T, 1) (T, 2) (T, 3) (T, 4) (T, 5) (T, 6)
   (b) $\frac{1}{12}$
5 (a)
```
Second spinner
 4 |  •       •       •
   |  (1,4)  (2,4)   (3,4)
 3 |  •       •       •
   |  (1,3)  (2,3)   (3,3)
 2 |  •       •       •
   |  (1,2)  (2,2)   (3,2)
 1 |  •       •       •
   |  (1,1)  (2,1)   (3,1)
 0 |__1_____2_____3___
            First spinner
```
   (b) $\frac{1}{12}$
   (c) (i) $\frac{1}{4}$ (ii) $\frac{1}{2}$ (iii) $\frac{1}{2}$

Exercise 6D

1 0.97
2 77%
3 (a) $\frac{3}{10}$ (b) $\frac{9}{10}$ (c) $\frac{7}{10}$ (d) 0
4 0.12
5 0.69
6 (a) $\frac{12}{25}$ (b) $\frac{1}{5}$ (c) $\frac{17}{25}$

Exercise 6E

1 (a) Black, since there is the least number of these.
   (b) $\frac{3}{10}$
   (c) (i) $\frac{2}{5}$ (ii) $\frac{7}{10}$ (iii) $\frac{11}{20}$ (iv) 0
2 (a) 0.996
   (b) Probability of being cracked = 0.004
       So the most likely number of eggs to be cracked
           = 140 000 × 0.004
           = 560 eggs

3 $\frac{14}{15}$
4 29 times
5 360 words

Exercise 6F

1 (a) (i) 0.2905 (ii) 0.176 (iii) 0.621
   (b) The company will need to ask more students, i.e. take a larger sample; this will make the estimates better.
2 (a) The outcome of the spinner is governed by the laws of chance, so it is likely that each time we spin the spinner 100 times we will get a different set of outcomes. So it is unlikely that Mandy will have 3 times the frequencies that John got.
   (b) (i) 0.1875 (ii) 0.5725
   (c) Our best estimates are P(A) = 0.1325
                              P(B) = 0.4275
                              P(C) = 0.1875
                              P(D) = 0.2525
       If the spinner was unbiased the probabilities would each be 0.25, so the spinner appears to be biased.
3 0.993
4 0.23
5 (a) The outcome of a coin toss is governed by the laws of chance, so it is likely that each time we toss a coin 100 times we will get a different number of heads.
   (b) 57 + 45 = 102
       Best estimate is P(H) = $\frac{102}{200}$ = 0.51
       If the coin is unbiased this probability should be about 0.5, so our estimate does not give sufficient evidence to suggest the coin is biased.

Mixed exercise 6

1 (a) $\frac{1}{10}$ (b) $\frac{3}{10}$ (c) $\frac{1}{10} + \frac{3}{10} = \frac{4}{10} = \frac{2}{5}$ (d) 0
2 (a) $\frac{3}{6} = \frac{1}{2}$ (b) $\frac{2}{6} = \frac{1}{3}$ (c) $\frac{1}{6}$ (d) 0
3 (a) (i) Blue
       (ii) There are 7 blue sections out of the total 12 sections.
   (b)
```
 ×
 |----|----|----|----|----|----|----|----|----|----|----|
 0   1/12 1/6  1/4  1/3  5/12 1/2  7/12 2/3  3/4  5/6  11/12  1
```
   (c) $\frac{4}{12} = \frac{1}{3}$
4 0.28 + 0.31 + 0.26 + 0.23 = 1.08
   But sum of probabilities = 1
   So there must be an error.
5 0.09
6 (a) $\frac{4}{12} = \frac{1}{3}$ (b) $\frac{9}{12} = \frac{3}{4}$ (c) 0 (d) $\frac{7}{12}$
7 $\frac{997}{1000}$
8 (a) 0.998 (b) 60
9 4%
10 (a) 0.2 (b) 0.48 (c) 0.55
11 (a) (i) $\frac{1}{6}$ (ii) $\frac{1}{2}$ (iii) $\frac{1}{3}$ (iv) 0
   (b) Ken's dice is biased. You would expect an unbiased dice to land with each face up ten times in sixty rolls. Ken's dice appears to be biased against 4 and towards 3.
12 They are not mutually exclusive events.
13 (win, win) (win, lose) (win, draw)
   (lose, win) (lose, lose) (lose, draw)
   (draw, win) (draw, lose) (draw, draw)

102 Answers

14 (a) (Red, 1) (Red, 2) (Red, 3) (Red, 4) (Red, 5)
(White, 1) (White, 2) (White, 3) (White, 4) (White, 5)
(Blue, 1) (Blue, 2) (Blue, 3) (Blue, 4) (Blue, 5)
(b) $\frac{1}{15}$

15 (wrap, chicken) (wrap, tuna) (wrap, cheese)
(wrap, ham) (wrap, hummus)
(baguette, chicken) (baguette, tuna) (baguette, cheese)
(baguette, ham) (baguette, hummus)
(bread, chicken) (bread, tuna) (bread, cheese)
(bread, ham) (bread, hummus)

16 (a)

	2nd spin		
1st spin	1	2	3
1	2	3	4
2	3	4	5
3	4	5	6

(b) (i) $\frac{1}{9}$ (ii) $\frac{2}{9}$ (iii) 0

17 (a) (i) 0.0375 (ii) 0.897 (3 s.f.)
(b) 276 500

18 (a) The outcome of the spinner is governed by the laws of chance, so it is likely that each time we spin it 100 times we will get a different set of outcomes. So it is unlikely Jenny will have twice the frequencies Michael had.
(b) (i) $P(B) = \frac{37}{150}$
(ii) $P(D) = \frac{1}{10}$
(iii) $P(\text{vowel}) = \frac{8}{25}$
(c) 100

19 If the spinner was not biased we would have $P(A) = P(B) = P(C) = P(D) = P(E) = 0.2$ i.e. we would expect each letter to come up about 2000 times. In fact, B came up 4009 times. A 593 times and C 1427 times, which suggests the spinner is biased in favour of B. It appears to be biased against A and, to a lesser degree, C.

Examination practice paper

Section A

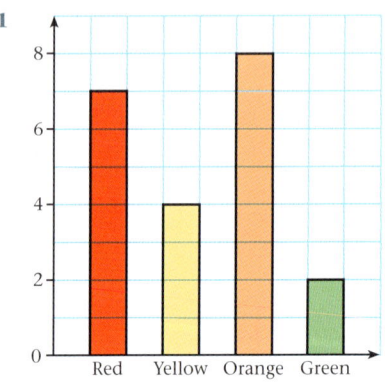

1

(bar chart: Red 7, Yellow 4, Orange 8, Green 2)

2 (a) 6 (b) 8 (c) 7

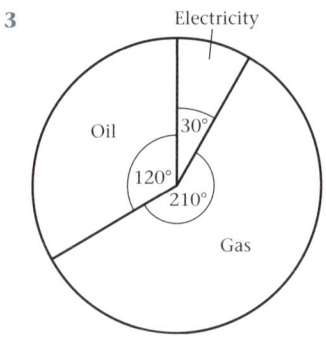

3

(pie chart: Electricity 30°, Gas 210°, Oil 120°)

4 (a) 0.55 (b) 0.45

Section B

1 (a)

Flavour	Tally	Frequency
Salt and vinegar	|||||	5
Cheese and onion	||||| |||	8
Plain	|||||		6
Bacon	|||||		6

(b) 6
(c) Cheese and onion

2 (a) B. There are more Bs than As or Cs
(b) $\frac{1}{6}$

3 The **mode** of a set of data is the value which occurs most often.
The **median** is the value in the middle when the values are listed in order of size.

4

	Badge	Flag	Sticker	Total
Male	27	**31**	23	81
Female	15	37	17	**69**
Total	**42**	68	**40**	150

5 (a), (c)

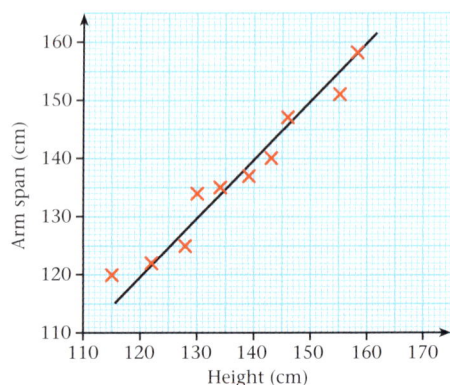

(scatter graph of Arm span (cm) vs Height (cm), positive correlation line of best fit)

(b) Positive correlation
(d) About 150 cm